Fandom Nationalism

BLOOMSBURY FANDOM PRIMERS

Series Editors

Paul Booth
Rukmini Pande

Previously published titles in this series:

The Construction of Race in Les Misérables *Fanworks*
Nemo Madeleine Sugimoto Martin

Romance Fandom in 21st-Century Pakistan
Javaria Farooqui

Fan Translations
Jonathan Evans and Ting Guo

Fandom Nationalism

Participatory Censorship and Performative Patriotism in East Asia

ERIKA NINGXIN WANG
AND QIAN HUANG

BLOOMSBURY ACADEMIC
NEW YORK • LONDON • OXFORD • NEW DELHI • SYDNEY

BLOOMSBURY ACADEMIC
Bloomsbury Publishing Inc, 1359 Broadway, New York, NY 10018, USA
Bloomsbury Publishing Plc, 50 Bedford Square, London, WC1B 3DP, UK
Bloomsbury Publishing Ireland, 29 Earlsfort Terrace, Dublin 2, D02 AY28, Ireland

BLOOMSBURY, BLOOMSBURY ACADEMIC and the Diana logo are
trademarks of Bloomsbury Publishing Plc

First published in the United States of America 2026

Cover design: Eleanor Rose
Cover image © J Studios / DigitalVision / Getty Images

A catalog record for this book is available from the Library of Congress.

ISBN: HB: 979-8-7651-2515-1
         PB: 979-8-7651-2516-8
       ePDF: 979-8-7651-2518-2
      eBook: 979-8-7651-2519-9

Series: Bloomsbury Fandom Primers

Typeset by Integra Software Services Pvt. Ltd.
Printed and bound in the United States of America

For product safety related questions contact productsafety@bloomsbury.com.

To find out more about our authors and books visit www.bloomsbury.com
and sign up for our newsletters.

All efforts were made to obtain permissions. For reasons of safety and security,
all interviewees are anonymous.

CONTENTS

FIGURES

ACKNOWLEDGMENTS

This book is a testament to the power of friendship, community, and shared stories. It emerged from a sweet afternoon tea session in London, took shape through our friendship, and is deeply rooted in the academic community we share. Together, we formed a synergy that carried us through the challenges of research and writing, each bringing unique perspectives that strengthened our work. We consider ourselves fortunate to have found such fulfilling collaboration in each other.

We owe profound gratitude to Professor Hye-Kyung Lee, whose mentorship and intellectual guidance shaped this project from its inception. Our colleagues at King's College London, the Chinese University of Hong Kong Shenzhen, the University of Groningen, and our wider academic community provided invaluable feedback that refined our thinking and enriched this work immeasurably.

At the heart of this book are the fan communities who opened their worlds to us, especially during the isolating times of the Covid-19 pandemic. To our interviewees who shared their experiences so candidly—your stories of passion, connection, and creativity form the soul of this research. You entrusted us with your laughter and tears, your triumphs and disappointments. Each conversation was a gift, and we treasure the memories of these exchanges. We hope our paths cross again in the continuing journey of fandom.

We extend our sincere gratitude to the series editors, Paul Booth and Rukmini Pande, whose vision provided a home for our work; to the anonymous reviewers whose thoughtful critiques strengthened our manuscript; and to the editorial team at Bloomsbury Academic for their expertise and dedication in bringing this book to publication.

This work exists because of countless contributions, conversations, and connections—some named here, others woven into the fabric of our academic and personal lives. To all who supported us along the way, our heartfelt thanks.

FOREWORD

What about China?

Henry Jenkins

In 2016, I was speaking at the London School of Economics at an event celebrating the release of *By Any Media Necessary: The New Youth Activism* (co-authored with Sangita Shresthova, Liana Gamber-Thompson, Neta Kligler-Vilenchik, and Arely M. Zimmerman). The book looks closely at multiple cases where networks and organizations had been able to recruit, train, and mobilize young activists to help foster meaningful social change and prolonged participation in civic and political processes. These new practices fuse the cultural and the political.

Similarly, Cathy J. Cohen and Joseph Kahne also reflect in a white paper,

> The participatory skills, norms and networks that develop when social media is used to socialize with friends or to engage with those who share one's interests can and are being transferred to the political realm ... what makes participatory culture unique is ... the shift in the relative prevalence of circulation, collaboration, creation and connection is changing the cultural context in which people operate.

And then, someone in the audience raised what I have come to think of—What about China? Is participatory culture capable of enabling voices beyond Western democracies?

I honestly don't recall what I said. I mumbled something that felt inadequate at the time. I was no China specialist, yet my gut told me that some of our concepts could have profound implications there. Having now spent more time on the ground in China, talking with Chinese fans and observing their practices, I see the stakes in even more vivid terms. As they say in social media, "it's complicated."

To unpack this more, we might start with the distinction between celebrity activism and fan activism. The first is top-down, tapping the heightened visibility and influence which celebrities enjoy in mass media and among their fans and followers. Taylor Swift endorses a candidate, BTS contributes to Black Lives Matter. By contrast, fan activism is bottom-up as fans tap their shared interests in fan objects as the starting point for forging communities that recruit, train, and mobilize around urgent issues. Trans Harry Potter fans call out J. K. Rowling, Hunger Games fans flash the three-finger salute in support of labor organizing; Palestinians paint themselves like Na'vi and march along the Gaza border.

We have since seen this model at work around the world: young people who often felt powerless within institutional politics fight for their perceived justice in ways they know best. We developed these ideas in a moment of heightened optimism, at the end of the Obama era when the American youth had voted in record numbers, in the midst of the Arab Spring and Occupy movements.

But not long after *By Any Media Necessary* was released, Donald Trump's MAGA movement emerged. The mechanisms of participatory politics proved not to be inherently democratic. New strong-men leaders around the globe operate as a new form of celebrity courting their followers as fans with such new civic skills to remain in power. We saw the deployment of many aspects of fan activism in the United States through the Q-Anon conspiracy theory and the attack on the US Capitol on January 6, 2021.

Fandom studies has had much to contribute to our understanding of these far-right movements—the ways they encouraged empowerment and entitlement through participation, linked culture and politics into potent mythologies, fostered new forms of expertise, and tapped skills acquired through recreation. "Toxic fandom" has become a high growth research topic as we seek to understand the rise of reactionary politics within the so-called Western democracies.

China re-entered my consciousness when an interview request came in March 2020 regarding the Chinese government's shutting down of Archive of Our Own (AO3) in the midst of a controversy surrounding fan fiction and *The Untamed*. The shutdown was the result of a conflict between different fandoms—one enjoying erotic fantasies about fictional characters and the other seeking to protect the reputation of the idols who played those characters.

My book, *Textual Poachers: Television Fan and Participatory Culture,* had recently been translated for the Chinese market and I was interviewed multiple times by Chinese media on relevant issues. But I felt inadequate, and progressively so as my understanding about what had happened there evolved and my grasp of Chinese fandom deepened. I knew that I would need to go to China, talk with Chinese fans, and understand what these events meant to them.

Several years later, I came to Shanghai University to teach a course on Western Fandom Studies. During my office hours, students shared their experiences as fans. One woman wept in my office and shared having written all her fan fiction as a teenager on a library computer before posting them online, so when AO3 and other fan fiction depositories were shut down, she lost everything she had ever written, a devastating experience. She urged me to keep speaking out and to share that story wherever I could.

I went into the shopping malls, attending fan gatherings, learning about their public expressive practices as cosplayers, seeing fan women's sociality when they experience films together and engage in intense discussions about gender and sexuality, and observing how fandom held open spaces for queer fans even within a homophobic society. Shanghai has one of the most intense, vital, creative, and public fan cultures I have observed anywhere in the world.

If China were going to change, fandom would be part of that change. Change in China would occur at the grassroots level: change in how people treated each other and how they imagined their place in the world. Chinese fans were encountering ideas about feminism, say, through their encounters with anime, K-pop, and Barbie, that would have a lasting impact upon their sense of themselves and the world.

But, again, this was only part of the picture.

I also hear about the state's increasing investment in shaping fandom in its own image. Fan conventions were increasingly brought under the control of the political infrastructure. The places where fans might rent and wear Hanfu costumes were influenced by the state in order to foster "cultural confidence," reversing policies under Mao which sought to destroy all traces of Chinese dynastic cultures. I hear about popular performers or media texts losing their followings overnight when creators made statements read as "anti-China." I hear about the "Little Pink" movement where large networks of fans take collective actions raiding fan sites in other countries to promote Chinese nationalism. This, too, was part of fan politics with Chinese characteristics.

All of this brings us to this book and its authors. While others have written about fan nationalism and some of its specific aspects, this book is the fullest and most nuanced discussion of fan nationalism in English that I have read. The authors spell out in clear terms the mechanisms by which the Chinese government seek to direct the energies of the fan community toward support of their national agenda and used it as a means of reshaping the identities of Chinese youth. They illustrate these mechanisms through close and prolonged attention to particular case studies. They offer us tools for analysis that could also be applied to understanding social movements around the world.

This is vital work that should be read by all of us in fandom studies. To understand what's occurring, we need to hold multiple seemingly contradictory things in our heads at the same time (fandom as a bottom-up mechanism of grassroots change, fandom as a top-down extension of state power). Without dismissing the agency of fans or its capacity for progressive change, we also need to recognize that fandom as a site of political socialization is also deployed in the interests of more conservative forces, whether the far-right movement or the nationalists.

This book illustrates the importance of cross-cultural dialogues around these urgent questions and the need for more collaborative and comparative work that incorporates global perspectives beyond Anglo-American fandoms and their specific fan subsets.

Introduction

In contemporary pop culture and societies in general, fandoms have demonstrated themselves as a formidable social force that mobilizes individuals and communities. Such force can not only be used for progressive social movements and activism (Jenkins 2006) but can also be wielded for less plausible causes such as fan wars, trolling, and some other toxic mobilization (Ng 2020). What will happen, then, if such force is combined with nationalism—another strong social mobilizing force—in a society with strong state intervention in cultural practices and a dominant national narrative of patriotism, such as China?

This is an understudied territory in fan studies. The dominant perspectives in fan studies, especially in the West, have been paying more attention to the democratic and civic engagement capacity in fan mobilization. However, such a narrative should be complicated as other forms of fan mobilization rise globally. As one of these above-mentioned fan mobilization forms, fandom nationalism is currently most visible in East Asian countries such as Korea (e.g., Jin 2021) and China (e.g., Liu 2019), but its significance and future implications transcend geographical boundaries. Compared to cancel culture, another form of fan mobilization that garnered much academic attention in the past years (Ng 2020; Norris 2023), fandom nationalism cases present more complex power dynamics between different stakeholders such as fans, digital platforms, mainstream media outlets, commercial interests, and the state.

This primer will guide you through the exploration of fandom nationalism in China to understand these dynamics and intricacies. Upon finishing this primer, you will be able to answer the following questions: What exactly does fandom nationalism entail? How to research fandom nationalism? How are fandoms mobilized in relation to nationalism on digital platforms under the watchful eye of state surveillance and censorship? We hope this primer ignites your interest in the un(der)explored phenomenon and dimensions of fandom nationalism.

The Rising Entanglement of Fandom and Nationalism

Recent years have witnessed a surge in online nationalist activities among the younger generation of Chinese social media users, a trend that has increasingly captured the attention of scholars. In 2016, Chinese nationalistic social media users went on a Diba Expedition: they adopted fandom-like practices and strategies to attack Tsai Ing-wen's (Taiwan's presidential candidate at that time and later president-elect) and several Taiwanese newspapers' Facebook pages by swarming their comments section with memes as their weapons of choice (Han 2015; Liu 2019). These strategies are perceived as successful in this incident, which led Chinese citizens to use the same strategies in several other incidents in the following few years (Liu 2019; Yang 2019). In many of these incidents, the mobilization was triggered by perceived transgressions from Japan and Western countries. Such sentiments in public opinion have also been demonstrated offline in various anti-Japan/South Korea/US protests, which not only align with the official nationalist narratives promoted by the Party-State but also in turn shape China's official foreign policies and diplomatic relationships (Liu 2006; Wu 2007). This dynamic also applies to digital nationalist mobilization (Han 2021).

Ever since, the Party-State has sought to engage such fandom-like collective actions as a key propaganda component. The participants involved do not necessarily belong to fandoms of specific cultural products or celebrities, but they apply the practices and strategies from fandom collective actions to defend China. Researchers (Liu 2019; Wang 2022) coined the term *fandom nationalism* to conceptualize how Chinese citizens and social media users demonstrate their love for the nation-state in the way of fans loving their idols. These participants become fans of the nation-state, seeking to purge all relevant negative comments on social media and feuding with all perceived enemies to the nation-state. Hereby, we provide Figure 0.1 and some more explanation to help you understand such a process.

In China, the Party-State provides a grand national narrative of patriotism, which promotes nationalist sentiments among Chinese citizens and the society in general. When Chinese citizens adopt the fandom-like collective actions to express patriotism, these collective actions promote pro-regime discourses that resonate with the official narratives of century-long national humiliation and the current national revival (Gries 2007) despite being grass roots movements.

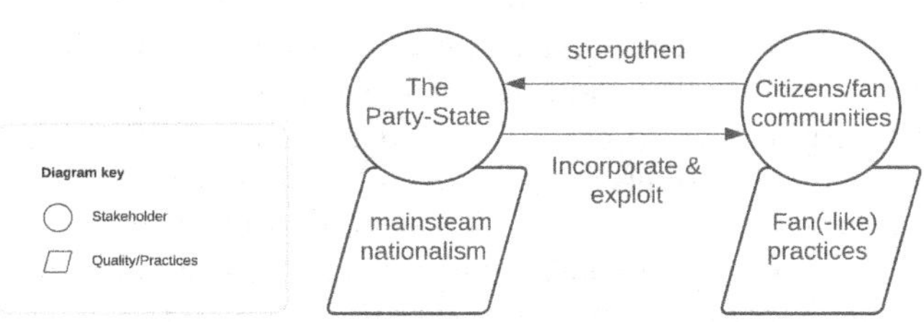

FIGURE 0.1 *Conceptualized fandom nationalism process in existing literature (e.g., Liu 2019; Jin 2021).*

Meanwhile, such intensified conflicts on social media platforms among individuals can also help divert and neutralize criticism toward the regime (Han 2015). Hence, these sentiments and collective actions are later incorporated and exploited by the state as a powerful weapon to strengthen nationalist narratives and propaganda.

Even though many researchers regard this phenomenon as fandom practices, not all Chinese citizens who participate in fandom nationalism are willing to claim the fan identity. Some may even perceive fan identities as exclusive to women and people with blind fanaticism, which does not align with their rational patriotism. For example, comments about this in the comment section under the news about fangirls' participation in national expeditions are very common, comments such as "do not let the term 'fangirl' contaminate our battle" (Weibo, accessed on August 25, 2021) and "[…] those brainless women are not the main force in the campaign; our brothers from the Diba are" (Weibo, accessed on August 25, 2021). Such gendered perception of fandom adds to the complexity of fandom nationalism, which warrants a more nuanced understanding of different communities and interactions involved in this phenomenon.

In addition, mainstream criticism intensifies the volatile and marginalized position of fandom and fan culture in China. In June 2021, the Cyberspace Administration of China (hereafter CAC) began the *Qinglang Xingdong* (Sweep-up Campaign), targeting online fan communities in China with the goal to clean up harmful collective actions in fandoms such as fan wars and fan conflicts at various levels. Fans are very much aware of such marginalization and their vulnerable position in Chinese society, which propels them to actively seek ways to align with mainstream ideologies and policies such as patriotism.

Therefore, many of such collective actions organized by fans in China in the past few years serve the following functions: to create a patriotic image of the idols and demonstrate that the idols have a positive influence on their fans, which ensure the safe existence and the potential flourishing of the idols and their fandoms. By actively showing their patriotism, the idols and their fandoms can avoid being questioned about their political stance and potentially being punished for un-patriotism by the Party-State or the mainstream society. These fandom practices and conventions are spontaneously formed and gradually become more widely recognized and practiced by almost all fan communities. These demonstrations and performances of patriotism are conducted by both idols and fans, which constitute a unique landscape where Chinese fan culture, mainstream nationalist sentiments, and state power interact. Similar dynamics can also be found in other sociopolitical contexts. For instance, BTS fans engaged in nationalist debates on social media to defend their idols when BTS Japanese fans strongly condemned one BTS Korean member for wearing a T-shirt depicting the atomic bomb explosion in Japan (Jin 2021). The nationalist sentiments shown by the Korean BTS fans went beyond ethnicities and mainly emerged from the intention to protect idols (Jin 2021).

Cases like this demonstrate how the transnational nature of fandoms complicates the interactions between nationalism and fandoms. Are fandom collective actions always in accordance with nationalist sentiments? If yes, how should we understand the roles that love toward idols and love toward nations play in mobilizing nationalist collective actions? If no, what will fans do when fan identities conflict with national identities or mainstream ideologies?

Bearing these intriguing questions in mind, we explore fandom dynamics in a long-term ethnography and then demonstrate some of these intricacies by zooming in on one specific incident. This allows us to develop a more nuanced conceptualization of the fandom nationalism process to show that not only can the state exploit nationalist fandom mobilizations but fandoms and commercial actors can also take advantage of the grand narrative of patriotism and public nationalist sentiments for their own and these idols' benefit.

Study Fandom Nationalism in the Digitized and Platformized Chinese Society

Chinese Fandom and Digital Cultures Afforded by Social Media Platforms

Since the 1990s, Chinese fan communities have evolved together with internet technologies (Zhang 2024). As the Chinese internet progresses from websites/forums to platforms, Chinese fandoms also undergo developments and changes regarding the main fan objects, practices, and relevant public discourses (Zhang 2024). Similar to Western scholars (e.g., Jenkins 2006; Hills 2013; Booth 2015; Stanfill 2019, 2024), Chinese fandom researchers gradually shift their focus from Chinese fandoms' civic potentials (e.g., Fung 2013; Zhang 2016) to their potential negative impact of mobilization (e.g., Luo and Li 2022; Shan and Chen 2021), struggles and negotiation under the state power (e.g., Wang and Ge 2022; Zheng 2024), and the exploitation of/within fandom economy (e.g., Sun 2020; Wu et al. 2025). In this process, Chinese fandom practices are increasingly afforded by, dependent on, and embedded in digital platforms: from the media texts they consume and identity and community construction to the operational practices and logic (Fung 2019; Zhang and Negus 2020; Cui and Wu 2024; Yin and Xie 2024). This primer focuses on Chinese fandoms' development in the past decade since 2014—also referred to as Phase 3 by Zhang (2024), where Sina Weibo became the key public platform of Chinese fandom interactions and operations.

Sina Weibo (thereafter Weibo) is the most dominant social media platform for public interactions in China and had over 590 million monthly active users in December 2024 (Sina Weibo 2025). It shares some similar fundamental features with X, such as follow, comment, repost, like, hashtag, and trending. However, it also developed unique features such as *chaohua* (Super Topic)[1] and its related points-earning system through daily check-ins, *resoubang* (ranking charts),[2] and *reping* (popular comments).[3] Afforded and shaped by these features of Weibo, Chinese fandoms have established various routine practices to improve their idols' visibility and commercial values (Yin 2020; Zhang and Negus 2020; Zhao and Chen 2023; Cui and Wu 2024; Yin and Xie 2024). The most common activities are as follows: *zuoshuju* (manipulating the data traffic about idols), which involves artificially inflating metrics such as views, likes, and shares to boost an idol's perceived popularity; *kongping* (managing comments), where fans collectively make positive comments and like them to push negative comments down and make them less visible, helping them win fan wars; *fanhei* (anti-criticism), where fans actively defend their idols against negative comments or criticism, often through coordinated efforts; and sales-data-driven consumption, where fans purchase products or services endorsed by their idols in bulk to demonstrate their support and enhance the idol's commercial appeal (Yin 2020; Zhang and Negus 2020; Zhao and Chen 2023; Cui and Wu 2024; Yin and Xie 2024). Weibo serves as a pivotal arena for idol fandom to convene, construct sub-communities, and cultivate idols' public images. Such fan activities range from sharing photographs and creating fan-generated cultural products to composing posts and participating in discussions with intentional and strategic usage of hashtags.

However, it is also important to note that the Chinese fandom economy is also embedded in a multi-platform ecology beyond Sina Weibo, which requires fans' intensive labor to navigate

---

[1]*Super Topics* are dedicated discussion spaces within the platform where users can engage in focused conversations around specific topics.

[2]*Ranking Charts* highlight trending topics and popular content based on user engagement and *reping* (popular comments).

[3]*Reping* highlights and shows the comments with the most likes at the top of the comments section under posts.

across platforms such as Taobao, Xianyu, Bilibili, Douyin, Douban, Xiaohongshu, WeChat, and QQ (Cui and Wu 2024; Wang 2024).[4] Compared to Weibo's hallmark features of relative anonymity and openness (Cui and Wu 2024; Wang 2024), WeChat, in contrast, constitutes a more intimate social media domain and personal networks afforded by its main features, such as friend requests and private as well as group chats (Shen and Gong 2018; Ou and Lin 2023). While these platforms have their own affordance, the principles and logic of contemporary Chinese fandom practices remain closely linked to platformization, datafication, and consumption capitalism. Similar dynamics between fan communities, fandom practices, and digital platforms are broadly observed in Asia, especially in transnational fandoms surrounding J-pop and K-pop.

A Plethora of Methods to Study Fandom Nationalism

In order to understand these fandom dynamics embedded in the digital platform ecosystems, researchers in fandom studies adopt a wide range of methods to study various aspects of fan practices on digital platforms. In this section, we will briefly introduce the major approaches taken in previous research about fandom nationalism so that you can learn about, choose from, and develop appropriate data collection and analysis methods for your own research project.

To identify patterns of large-scale or general fandom practices, some researchers adopt quantitative methods in

---

[4]Taobao and Xianyu are e-commerce platforms where fans can purchase relevant merchandise to demonstrate their idols' commercial value. Bilibili, Douyin, Douban, and Xiaohongshu are other public social media platforms where fans can post and comment on idol-related content to improve their idols' data performance, too. WeChat and QQ are private messaging platforms where fan communities can communicate and organize individually or in group chats.

their case studies. For collecting data, digital methods such as scraping social media posts, comments, and metadata via API (Wang 2018; Wang and Luo 2022; Chen and Gao 2023) are widely used. Such data can include not only textual content (e.g., posts and comments) but also relevant metadata such as timestamp, account, the number of likes/reposts, IP locations, etc. Researchers usually conduct regression analysis and topic modeling on collected data (Wang and Luo 2022; Chen and Gao 2023). Another common set of quantitative methods is analysis of online surveys, through which researchers explore the statistical relationship between consumption, perceptions, motivations, identities, and practices (Devlin et al. 2020; Liao et al. 2022; He and Li 2023).

While the number of researchers adopting quantitative and computational methods is increasing, most fandom researchers conduct qualitative research—the more conventional approach in cultural studies—to understand the lived experiences of fan communities. Researchers collect such data through semi-structured in-depth interviews with fans (Lyan 2019; Dong et al. 2022; Wang and Luo 2022; Chew 2023; Leung 2023), manually acquiring social media posts/comments (Han 2015; Zhou and Miao 2018; Gong 2022; Lam and Zhou 2023; Cui 2025), selecting relevant media texts such as films and amines (Guan and Hu 2020; Guo 2023; Huang and Lams 2024), as well as ethnographies (Chen 2017; Lee and Abidin 2022; Wang 2022; Song 2023). Depending on the goals of individual research, researchers choose from appropriate analysis methods. Grounded theory and inductive thematic analysis are usually adopted to identify main patterns thematically in collected data (Han 2015; Chen 2017; Wang 2022). Discourse analysis is often conducted to reveal ideologies and power dynamics behind nationalist communicative and media texts (Zhou and Miao 2018; Guan and Hu 2020; Guo 2023; Cole 2024), including more specific approaches such as multimodal discourse analysis (Huang and Lam 2024) and critical discourse analysis (Jin 2021; Kang 2023; Cui 2025).

In addition to the aforementioned methods, some researchers also adopt mixed-methods approach, which is largely due to the complexity of fandom nationalism dynamics. Depending on the research scope and questions, researchers can choose to mix data collection (e.g., quantitative and qualitative, interview and media texts) and/or data analysis methods.

For this primer specifically, we adopt a mix of long-term and immersive digital and multi-sited ethnography where we conduct mainly participant observation and in-depth interviews (Silverman 2015) (see Figure 0.2).[5] This ensures that we highlight fans' personal experiences as individuals and communities as ethnography is helpful to examine the practices of real people in their daily lives through participant observation (Kottak 2002; Booth and Williams 2021). As Ingold explains, in the conduct of the ethnographic research, "we meet people,

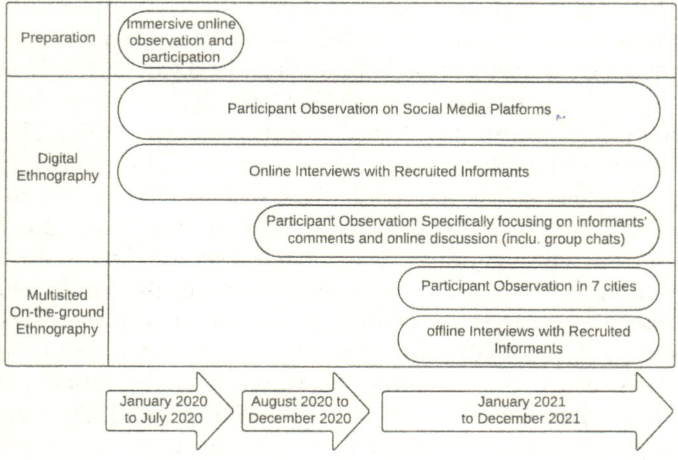

FIGURE 0.2 *Research stages and methods.*

---

[5]For consistency, "we/our/us" is used for writing this primer, but please note that the ethnography and other forms of data collection are conducted by the first author, Dr. Erika Ningxin Wang alone.

we talk with them, we ask them questions, we listen to their stories and we watch what they do" (2014, 385). Our digital ethnography follows the anthropologist Daniel Miller's (2018) digital anthropology approach and the specific interpretation of digital ethnography research methods proposed by Wang and Liu (2021). Following their approaches, we combine participatory observation about how digital technologies are used in fans' on-the-ground participation and fans' practices and interactions on digital platforms.

The digital technologies central to our digital ethnographic inquiry are two Chinese social media platforms: Weibo and WeChat, as they are the preeminent social media platforms among Chinese fans, as explained before. Our digital ethnography data includes:

1. the general observation of publicly accessible content posted on Weibo (January 2020 to December 2021);[6]

2. the targeted and consented observation of our informants' Weibo posts, discussions, daily tasks, interactions (December 2020 to December 2021);

3. the consented observation of our informants' WeChat groups' daily discussions.[7]

Our long-term ethnography started with general BL fandom. BL is short for "Boys' Love."[8] During the fieldwork period, two BL-adapted dramas dominated the Chinese

---

[6]This type of data collection falls under the purview of the KCL ethics committee's approval (the first author's affiliated institution at the time): permission to acquire without seeking explicit consent from the content originators.

[7]Parts 2 and 3 data collection obtained ethical approval (LRS-20/21-20160) from King's College London ethics committee in December 2020.

[8]BL originated as a genre of Japanese manga in the 1970s, featuring "love, sex and romance between boys and young men" and has been transformed into different forms of cultural texts (Martin 2012, 365). BL cultural texts have garnered popularity as well as censorship since the early 2000s in China (Hu et al. 2024a, 2024b).

market and generated a large number of fans: the earlier one *Chen Qing Ling* (*The Untamed*) was aired in 2019 and the later one *Shanhe Ling* (*The Word of Honor*) was aired in 2021. As they are both BL-adapted dramas during this period, there is a significant overlap in these two fandoms, and many informants discuss examples and their participation in both fandoms. Therefore, while our case study is primarily about Zhang Zhehan, whose stardom was made in *The Word of Honor*, our analysis involves observations and data about fandom practices related to both *The Word of Honor* and *The Untamed*.

The inclusion of overlapping data reflects our approach of centering fans rather than fan objects. As fieldwork progressed, we observed the fluidity of fan identities and the dynamics within BL fan communities. Fans often engage with multiple fan objects—such as the BL-adapted dramas *The Untamed* and *The Word of Honor*—traverse various communities, and maintain multiple fandom identities. This led us to follow fans' paths of engagement rather than restricting data to specific fan objects, as their rituals, dialogues, and practices transcend individual fan objects. For example, some fans transitioned from *The Untamed*'s fandom to *The Word of Honor*'s fandom, later becoming CP-fans, only-fans, or anti-fans of Zhang. Interviews and observations revealed frequent cross-references to practices in other fandoms. Excluding data based on fan objects would have been restrictive, failing to capture the multifaceted nature of fan culture. By centering fans, we account for the fluidity and consistency of broader fan practices.

The six-month preparatory immersion (January–July 2020) involved registering two Weibo accounts to join fan clubs, establish fan identities, and build friendships within the community. We engaged organically with fans, participating in bromance fantasies, creating fan-generated content, and attending fan events. This period was crucial for understanding the community's rules, hierarchy, division of labor, and lexicon.

Insider knowledge is explained in footnotes, and glossaries are provided for reference.

During recruitment, we introduced our research to fan friends, emphasizing its potential to authentically represent fan culture. Given mainstream misunderstandings of fandom, fans welcomed the opportunity to be understood without bias. This resonated with many, leading to seven initial informants who consented to face-to-face interviews. Through snowball sampling, informants introduced us to others in their fan circles, expanding our pool. By May 2021, we reached data saturation with twenty-five informants, though some opted out of participation.

The subsequent phases focused on Zhang's incident, detailed in Chapter 2. Data included insights from twenty-five informants' social media accounts, WeChat group discussions, participation in on-the-ground fan events, and face-to-face or video interviews. We maintained long-term communication with informants to track their evolving thoughts and experiences. A list of pseudonymized informants is provided in the appendix. The mixed digital and on-the-ground data collection allowed us to triangulate informants' thoughts, actions, and self-reported behaviors, avoiding the online-offline binary and providing a nuanced understanding of contemporary Chinese fan culture.

Our digital ethnography is centered on Weibo and WeChat. Weibo was the primary site for establishing contacts, building fan identities, integrating into communities, and participating in online discussions. We then transitioned to WeChat for more intimate observations of group discussions and in-depth interviews. On Weibo, we took screenshots, saved media, and maintained handwritten field notes, dedicating 2–3 hours daily to observing fan discussions, completing tasks, and monitoring platform administrators. During Zhang's controversies (August 12–19, 2021), observation increased to twelve hours daily. On WeChat, we obtained informed consent before observing group chats and conducting interviews.

Multi-sited on-the-ground fieldwork spanned seven Chinese cities (Beijing, Tianjin, Guangzhou, Shanghai, Suzhou, Changsha, and Hengdian) from December 2020 to December 2021. Stays ranged from two weeks to two months, with repeat visits to Guangzhou, Shanghai, Changsha, Hengdian, and Suzhou for fan events and in-person interviews.

Conducting ethnographic research in fandom requires careful ethical consideration, focusing on three main concerns: participants' well-being, the impact of researchers' entry into the field, and power dynamics between researchers and participants (Ingold 2014). To safeguard fans' privacy, safety, and consent, we implemented several measures:

1. Engaging only with adult informants (18+).
2. Using exclusively publicly accessible information for online observations.
3. Anonymizing or pseudonymizing informants and obscuring faces in photographs.
4. Translating and paraphrasing posts in English to prevent traceability.
5. Discarding or obscuring details that could expose informants' identities.
6. Obtaining informed consent for all observations and interviews.

Researchers' authoritative positions and proximity to fans' daily lives can disrupt their interactions and behaviors (Hills 2013; Booth 2017). Fans might conceal taboo aspects of their identities, such as fantasies about male idols' sexuality. To minimize interference, we adopted an "aca-fan" role (Jenkins 1992), combining academic research with fan identity. This shared experience fostered trust and rapport, enabling respectful and authentic exploration of the community (Miller 2018).

Initially, we aimed to exclude personal friends to preserve objectivity. However, long-term fieldwork in China led to close friendships with informants over two years. These relationships allowed candid sharing of personal experiences challenging mainstream values, with informants viewing us as spokespersons for their fandom. This highlights the importance of the aca-fan role in aligning with informants' desire for genuine representation.

While these connections enhanced access to authentic data, they also introduced complexities. As fans, we experienced the emotional intensity of fandom—joy, conflict, and cyberbullying. Balancing emotional involvement with scholarly detachment posed a unique challenge, as our personal experiences inevitably intertwined with academic rigor. Navigating this dualism of empathy and objectivity remains a distinctive aspect of our role as aca-fan ethnographers.

Roadmap of the Primer

In previous sections, we briefly presented how fandoms and nationalism interacted in China, an overview of how researchers study these dynamics, as well as our main research questions and methods. In the following chapters, we will provide more details of fandom nationalism as a rising phenomenon in East Asia, introducing our case study of Zhang's cancellation; explain how the concepts of participatory censorship and performative patriotism can be applied to understanding fandom nationalism; and, ultimately, propose a preliminary model to understand the practices and interactions between different stakeholders in fandom nationalism incidents—and potentially cancel culture incidents in certain contexts.

By reviewing a rich body of literature related to the phenomenon of fandom nationalism in Chapter 1, we illustrate how this term has been defined and analyzed differently in contexts of J-pop, K-pop, and their fandoms in China. We also trace back to some relevant concepts (e.g., nation branding, pop nationalism, fan nationalism) that contribute to our understanding of the dynamics between pop culture fandoms and the state.

In Chapter 2, we dive into the case study of Zhang's cancellation: what happened and how it happened. We first demonstrate how fan wars can form in BL fandoms, which sets the background for you to understand later chapters. We then provide a chronological account of how Zhang became a target of nationalistic criticism as well as being boycotted and banned by the media and authorities.

Chapter 3 mainly focuses on the seemingly paradoxical fan practice demonstrated in Zhang's cancellation case and incidents alike: participation and censorship. Instead of treating them as a dichotomy, we will introduce and develop the concept of participatory censorship. Drawing from literature about the debates regarding cancel culture and scholarly discussion about Chinese citizens' peer surveillance and self-censorship in cultural industries, we argue that fandom nationalism demonstrates a form of fan participation practices where citizens voluntarily engage in, with the intention to control discourses, information flows, and/or the development of (fandom) incidents while aligning with the interests, narrative, values, and norms of power holders, the Chinese Party-State in this case. We then go back to our ethnographic data to show the dynamics between three crucial stakeholders in fandom nationalism—fans, nationalist citizens, and the Party-State—and how such participatory censorship is achieved and its impact in Zhang's incident.

After approaching fandom nationalism as participatory censorship, we then move on to Chapter 4 to interrogate the "sincerity" of the patriotism demonstrated in this process, where we also identify another type of key stakeholders—the businesses—and disentangle their interactions and dynamics in fandom nationalism cases like Zhang's incident. Inspired and informed by scholarly discussions about contemporary performative allyship/activism in the economy of visibility and Goffman's conceptualization of performativity, we introduce another concept, performative patriotism, to analyze fandom nationalism demonstrated in our case study. By using this concept, we highlight the intention of transforming garnered social media visibility and capital behind businesses' and fans' performative display and ritualistic affirmation of the Chinese identity and national pride.

After reading Chapters 3 and 4, you will understand how fans express their dedication to the state in ways that mirror their adoration for cultural idols, intertwining their love and hatred through collective actions like mass reporting and censorship. Chinese social media users' nationalist expressions in incidents of celebrities' cancellation have become a bridge where fan identities and practices meet the state's nationalist narratives. Adding to the complexity, various stakeholders try to align with mainstream nationalism in order to take advantage of the state power: fans use nationalist expression to fight for their idols, celebrities perform patriotism, and entertainment companies and media outlets stir up controversies and public emotions.

At the end of this primer, we will integrate the findings—practices, stakeholders, dynamics, and concepts—and present a model developed based on our analysis of participatory censorship and performative patriotism for you to understand similar incidents in the future. You can have a sneak peek into this model in Figure 0.3. We believe that this model can work as a base to understand fan mobilization practices that involve dominant ideologies and asymmetrical power relations in different contexts, beyond our specific case study, the Chinese context, and fandom cultures in East Asia.

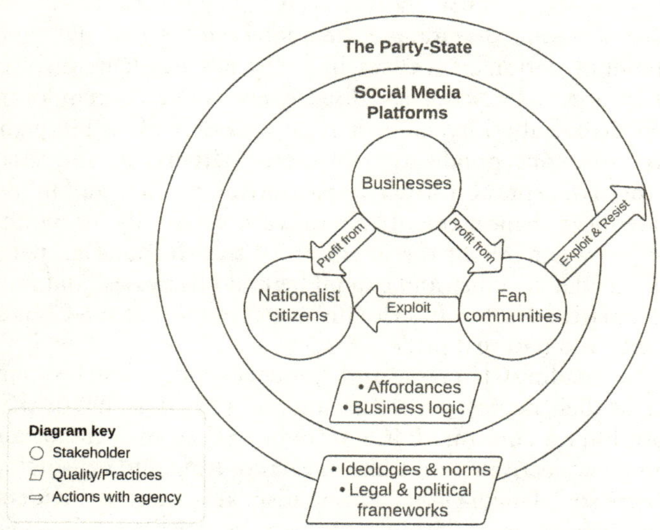

FIGURE 0.3 *Multi-stakeholder model of fandom nationalism in China.*

CHAPTER ONE

The Paths to Contemporary Fandom Nationalism in China

East Asian Pop Culture Fandoms and Nationalism

While the concept of fandom nationalism has more often been used to analyze the recent development of increasingly entangled pop culture fandoms and nationalism in China, relevant sentiments and dynamics have been studied by J-pop and K-pop researchers earlier. As early as 2005, Iwabuchi discusses how Japanese popular cultural products—such as anime and manga—shape international perceptions of Japan and transform global cultural flows. This forms Japan's transnationalism as Japanese popular culture is entangled with issues of identity, race, and politics, especially in relation to Japan's position in Asia and the broader world (Iwabuchi 2002). This way of shaping a country's global image is also often termed as soft power, nation branding, or cultural diplomacy. With Japan's success in improving its global reputation through its transnational flows of popular culture, South Korea seeks similar paths.

The Korean government promoted Hallyu—also known as the Korean Wave—to induce other nationals' positive dispositions toward itself. Such statecraft includes various types of pop cultural products, especially K-drama and K-pop (Kim 2022; Yoon 2023). In addition to seeking transnational popularity through attractive productions, nationalism is explicitly glamorized in K-dramas like *Jewel in the Palace* (2003) and *Descendants of the Sun* (2016). Such a formula is welcomed by Korean state leaders as this type of content could boost citizen loyalty to the country and legitimize the ruling party's political control (Leung 2021). Celebratory discourses of K-pop are commonly observed in Korean news media and public, reinforcing nationalism among domestic audiences (Yoon 2023). As Hallyu achieves more global impact, Korean public's nationalistic pride grows, which replaces the past's nationalistic fear of foreign cultural invasion. Korean researchers coined this phenomenon as pop nationalism, which views the Korean Wave phenomenon within nationalistic discourses and interests and attempts to appropriate transnationalizing Korean popular culture and achieve cultural prominence in globalization (Kim 2007; Joo 2011).

Just as nationalist sentiments in other countries, the nationalism in Korea expressed via and shaped by Hallyu manifests in aggressions toward "the others," which is the other side of the coin of the collective pride of Korean pop cultures and the nation-state. In various media texts, Koreans display, indulge, and fuel racial prejudice against others, especially people from developing countries (Han 2015). There have been several cases where K-pop celebrities are criticized for their blackfacing acts (Han 2015). In addition, Korea K-pop fans sometime are also confronted with the conflict between their national and fandom identities, just like their Chinese counterpart. In 2019, a trade dispute occurred between Korea and Japan. Combined with the troubled histories between the two countries, domestic anti-Japanese sentiments were heightened in South Korea. Several K-pop fandoms demanded that entertainment agencies cancel upcoming concerts in Japan. In this case, Korean fans challenged dominant pop nationalism discourses and aligned with mainstream nationalism by demanding collective patriotism from the K-pop industry (Kang 2023). This identity and nationalism negotiation and its impact on the cultural industries can also be observed in Korea's *Oegugin* (foreigner) YouTuber industry (Lee and Abidin 2022): "only the visually-compliant (i.e., White-presenting), politically-obedient (i.e., does not question racism in Korea), and commercially-viable (i.e., able to leverage on global interest in K-cultures) are able to succeed in the industry" (555).

Adding to the complexity of nationalism shaped by the globalization of Hallyu, the imagined community (Anderson 2006) goes beyond its national borders and Korean ethnicity/nationality. This is what Lyan (2019) and Jin (2021) conceptualize as fandom nationalism, which is very different from how Chinese researchers use this concept—we will elaborate on this in the next section. These two scholars conceptualize fandom nationalism as the process by which fans form imagined nation-states around cultural icons (e.g., K-pop groups like BTS) or movements (e.g., Hallyu), transcending traditional political nationalism in favor of a cultural and moral community. Unlike conventional nationalism, which is tied to political sovereignty, fandom nationalism operates through emotional investment, digital platforms, and transnational fan activism, creating a sense of belonging beyond geographic and ethnic boundaries. Lyan (2019) and Jin (2021) demonstrate fandom nationalism through distinct but interconnected case studies. Jin examines BTS's global fandom (ARMY) as an example of digital cyber-nationalism, where fans function as a transnational, self-organized "nation-state." Through coordinated social media campaigns, ARMY mobilizes to defend BTS from criticism, amplify their music, and even engage in socio political activism (e.g., fundraising for Black

Lives Matter), mirroring the collective identity and solidarity of a sovereign entity. Meanwhile, Lyan's study of Hallyu fan-nationalism reveals how non-Korean fans of K-pop and K-dramas adopt cultural proxies of Korean identity, such as studying the language or advocating for Korea's global image, to counteract local stigma associated with their fandom. Unlike traditional diasporic nationalism, which relies on ethnic ties, these fans construct belonging through emotional investment in Korean culture, positioning themselves as cultural insiders rather than passive consumers. Together, these cases show how fandom nationalism transcends geopolitical boundaries, replacing state-centric loyalties with digitally mediated, culturally rooted communities of belonging.

Hallyu researchers demonstrate how digital technologies have transformed nationalism into an affective and participatory phenomenon, where emotions and fan-driven mobilization challenge Western-centric cultural hegemony (Kim 2022). As a state-backed project of soft power or cultural diplomacy, Hallyu successfully creates a decentralized and intra-Asia transnational cultural flow. However, this success has also sparked tensions in other countries such as China and Japan, where the anti-Korean backlash clearly demonstrates the potential frictions in pop/fandom nationalism in transnational capitalist cultural industries.

The Development of Fandom Nationalism in China

As explained in the earlier section, the concept of fandom/ fan nationalism is used by K-pop researchers to understand how fans form imagined nation-states around cultural icons that transcend traditional political nationalism (Lyan 2019; Jin 2021). Coincidentally, around the same time, an emerging research field that centers on the phenomenon and concept of fandom nationalism and the interplay between fandom and nationalism in China was also established. By reviewing a wide range of relevant literature, we distinguish three main approaches to understand fandom nationalism in China.

The first approach highlights the tensions between fandom and national (or other political) identities in the inter-Asia transnational flows, where fans have to transcend their own grounded nationality to identify foreign culture and characters (Huat 2004; Chin and Morimoto 2013). While Korean and Japanese pop cultures have formed large Chinese fan bases, these fans' attitudes and interactions fluctuate with the shifting economic and diplomatic relationships between the three East Asian countries (Chen 2017). For example, some Chinese K-pop fans try to defend the compatibility between their taste and love of the nation by highlighting their idols' professionalism, but sometimes align with official nationalism over issues regarding historical and geopolitical conflicts (Gong 2022; Wang 2022). Their unexpected consent to the Hallyu ban in 2016, where K-pop idols' presence is banned in official Chinese mainstream media, is a demonstration of such negotiation (Gong 2022). In addition, the fear or resentment of "cultural invasion" also drives fandom nationalism, which can be seen in some Chinese social media users' negative attitude toward *Squid Game*'s popularity (Wang 2022).

Most of the current research on Chinese fandom nationalism follows the second approach set by Liu's (2019) edited volume surrounding the case study of Diba Expedition. In this approach, fandom nationalism is mainly studies regarding how fandom practices have been adopted by Chinese nationalists and/or how fan communities can be co-opted by the state to reinforce nationalism (Zhang 2016; Schneider 2023). In 2016, Chinese social media users aimed to collectively defend Chinese sovereignty by attacking the pro-independence of Taiwan on Facebook with the coordinated meme war. These practices draw on and appropriate fandom cultures to mobilize nationalism (Liu 2019; Zhuang et al. 2023; Wu and Fitzgerald 2024). Researchers who study this incident and incidents alike argue collectively to show

how social media platforms (both their visual, textual, and technological) allow nationalist social media users to construct narratives, express emotions, and reinforce ideologies through fandom-like practices and/or existing fan communities (Lams and Zhou 2023; Song 2023). Due to the observed effectiveness of this form of mobilization, the state started to adopt these strategies on social media platforms. Such strategies are not always successful and universally effective on all Chinese fans or citizens. For instance, the state-sponsored virtual idols "Jiangshangjiao" and "Hongqiman" underwent backlash and resistance on Weibo (Cui 2025). Liao and colleagues (2022) also find that the direct effects between fans' affection toward idols and nationalist sentiments are only significant if individual fans participate in online fan communities.

As Chinese fan cultures, digital platforms, and nationalism keep evolving, more researchers approach the phenomenon by investigating how Chinese fandom communities and fan cultures gradually internalize the ideology of nationalism as well as the surrounding social institutions. This can be observed among fans, celebrities, and cultural producers. For example, Chinese idol fans actively employ nationalist rhetoric—such as pride in the nation, collective belonging, and heroic sacrifices during the pandemic—to align their idols with state-endorsed values. By framing idol promotion as a form of "positive energy," they signal loyalty to national identity in order to ensure their idols' participation in state-organized events or official media campaigns. In so doing, fans participate in nationalism through their idols' persona construction by engaging with state-backed initiatives (Wang and Luo 2022). As for celebrities, it has become a common practice to signal their political loyalty on social media platforms, among which younger celebrities with more followers tend to repost from official accounts more often. This trend clearly shows that, through the convergence of state agendas, celebrity cultural power, and social media reach, the state dominates online discourse by turning popular culture into a key tool of political legitimation (Chen and Gao 2023). Similar adaptation can also be identified in Chinese animation and many other cultural producers. They learn to walk on tightropes to balance their need to attract and maintain fans while appeasing the state's hegemony (Guan and Hu 2020; Guo 2023). These dynamics and negotiations are not only observed in pop idol fandoms but also sports fandoms (Wang 2024; Zhang et al. 2024).

The aforementioned literatures that shed light on the dynamics between pop culture fandom and nationalism in China and East Asia have built a diverse and solid foundation for further investigation and conceptualization of fandom nationalism. From the next chapter onward, we will zoom in on our empirical case study to illustrate and conceptualize this phenomenon.

CHAPTER TWO

Fan Mobilization and Nationalism in Action

The Chinese Communist Party (CCP) has a long history of using mass entertainment to engage and educate the public for political and ideological purposes (Cai 2016). With the rapid expansion of China's media and entertainment industries after joining the World Trade Organization (WTO), the regulation of celebrities became a significant policy focus starting in 2005 (Xu and Yang 2021). This shift is evident through numerous official notices, policies, and laws, such as the Sweep-up Campaign launched by the Cyberspace Administration of China (CAC) in 2016, specifically aimed at regulating entertainment celebrities and their cultural products. One major theme of these regulations and official campaigns targeting the entertainment industry is patriotism. Against this backdrop, the incident surrounding Zhang is a fascinating example of the complex relationship between patriotic citizens, fans, and state authorities.

During the Covid-19 pandemic, nationalistic feelings surged online, fueled by China's successful handling of the pandemic (Schneider 2021). This rise in patriotism set the stage for an intense boycott of Zhang Zhehan, a popular male star in China. Following the massive success of *The Untamed* in 2020, a BL-adapted costume drama, and the rise of Xiao Zhan as a top superstar, businesses increasingly invested in BL-adapted dramas. Zhang Zhehan became another major star with the success of his BL-adapted drama *The Word of Honor* in March 2021. However, in 2021, anti-fans discovered photos Zhang had posted in 2018 from a visit to the Yasukuni Shrine in Japan, a site with deep historical controversy. These anti-fans quickly accused Zhang of being a *hanjian* (national traitor) on social media. Even though Zhang apologized on Weibo on August 13, 2021, expressing regret for his ignorance and reaffirming his patriotism, the public reaction remained harsh. Comments on the official accounts of brands he endorsed questioned the brands' political loyalties, prompting over twenty brands to end their contracts with him (ifeng 2021).[1] On August 14, music platforms removed his songs, and the video platform Youku deleted his name from the credits of his TV dramas. Douyin (the Chinese domestic version of TikTok) also banned Zhang's account the same day (ifeng 2021). The China Association of Performing Arts joined the boycott on August 15, urging member companies to follow suit. Simultaneously, Zhang's fan club and super topic platform were banned on Weibo, along with his and his studio's Weibo accounts. Anti-fans and fervent online nationalists celebrated this as a major victory, calling themselves the *chujiandui* (Traitor Eradication Squad).

Since the release of *The Word of Honor* in March 2021, thirteen out of our twenty-five informants shared lively discussions about this drama on their Weibo accounts. Among these thirteen fans, four eventually lost interest, but the others continued their engagement in different ways. Silvia, Rose, Tina, and Yumi became dedicated fans of Zhang Zhehan. Hailey, on the other hand, became a fan of Gong Jun, the other lead actor. Meanwhile, Penny, Karen, Quella, and Flora embraced both actors as a couple, often referred to as CP-fans. Interestingly, fans of *The Untamed* (Iris, Ole, Elly, and Meg) viewed *The Word of Honor* as a competitor to their beloved drama, perceiving its popularity as a threat to their idols' status. This led to them spreading rumors about the new drama

---

[1]https://ent.ifeng.com/c/88fnXtl9zmM (Retrieved September 29, 2021).

and its lead actors. It is important to note that fans often have multiple identities within different fan communities.

Additionally, we had informal chats with five fans of other idols (Zoe, Bella, Abby, Celia, and Wendy), where we exchanged third-person perspectives on the incident involving Zhang. Our extra fieldwork from August to September 2021 focused on observing the practices and thoughts of these thirteen fan informants. For this case study, we used two main approaches to gather data through online observation. First, the first author conducted digital ethnography from August to December 2021, observing discussions about the case on their informants' Weibo accounts, as well as the Weibo accounts of Zhang, his studio, the shows and dramas he was involved in, the brands he endorsed, and key official and entertainment media accounts. Second, we collected relevant news reports and comments from official media and responses on other platforms like Bilibili to supplement and cross-check these Weibo observations.

A notable event was the cast concert of *The Word of Honor* held in Suzhou on May 4, 2021, which drew over 20,000 fans. We conducted offline participant observation at this concert, recording both visual and written notes about the fans' homosexual fantasies and interactions among different fan sub-communities. We also had casual conversations with our thirteen informants involved in this fan conflict. Given the politically sensitive nature of the incident, a formal interview format might have made them uncomfortable. Our conversations were spontaneous, taking place in voice calls and face-to-face chats, focusing on their personal feelings and assessments of the event rather than passing judgment on the Zhang scandal.

Rivalries and Fan Wars

The story kicks off with an intriguing anonymous exposé, fueled by the surge in popularity of the BL-adapted drama *The Word of Honor*. Following its debut in March 2021, the drama's lead actors, Zhang Zhehan and Gong Jun, quickly became favorites among CP-fans—a community of fans who celebrate and fantasize about a romantic relationship between their favorite characters or actors. Among my informants, thirteen became devoted CP-fans of the Gong–Zhang pairing. They eagerly shared with me the 'sweets'[2] they had collected—slang used by CP-fans for clues of romance they observe between the actors. The excitement among the fans culminated during a concert associated with the drama in Suzhou on May 4, 2021. The interactions on stage—talks, songs, and hugs between Zhang and Gong—were viewed by fans as undeniable "evidence" of the actors' romantic relationship. The atmosphere was perceived as electric and led to a fan-organized "marriage ceremony" for the two actors outside the venue. They displayed large shiny signs bearing the names of Zhang and Gong, alongside a massive heart-shaped LED decoration.

As demonstrated in the captured photos (see Figure 2.1 and Figure 2.2), the ceremony drew a crowd of over 5,000 people, consisting of predominantly excited CP-fans equipped with banners, fan-made merchandise, and mobile phones that enabled them to capture every moment of this fake yet symbolic wedding.

The vibrant world of CP-fans, who had been united in their adoration for the romantic pairing of Zhang Zhehan and Gong Jun, was then suddenly thrown into disarray. The drama unfolded when anti-fans unearthed private photos from a friend's social media where Zhang was seen in an intimate pose with a woman. These images, quickly spread by his detractors, sparked accusations of dishonesty and unprofessionalism. Critics claimed Zhang was misleading fans by portraying himself as a potential gay partner while being involved with a woman, given his role in a BL-adapted drama.

---

[2]Eating sweets is a commonly used jargon among CP fans, which signifies the act of deriving implicit romantic cues from the interactions between the idols being paired.

FIGURE 2.1 *At the entrance of the Suzhou concert on May 4, 2021, CP-fans held up flashing banners saying, "Jun and Zhe getting married," prompting many CP-fans to take photos. The photo was taken by the first author during fieldwork.*

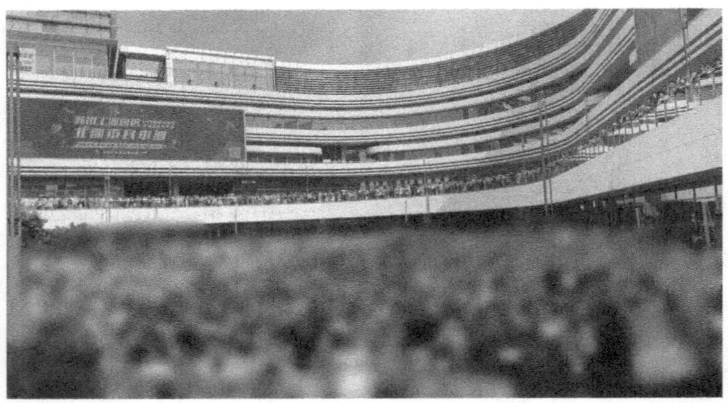

FIGURE 2.2 *At the entrance of the Suzhou concert on May 4, 2021. The photos were taken by the first author during fieldwork.*

This scandal shattered the once joyous atmosphere among our thirteen CP-fan informants. The group, which had eagerly shared and celebrated every sweet moment between the duo, found itself deeply divided. Four informants, disillusioned by the revelations, abandoned the fandom entirely. Another informant shifted allegiance to become solely a fan of Gong Jun, distancing herself from Zhang Zhehan. Four chose to support Zhang exclusively, while the remaining four continued to cherish the Gong–Zhang pairing despite the controversy.

This split turned their WeChat group from a harmonious gathering into a battleground of conflicted loyalties and tensions. In June 2021, just a month after their grand "wedding ceremony," which was a peak moment in their fandom, the fractures deepened. Hailey, one of the original CP-fans, decided to support Gong alone, feeling betrayed by Zhang's perceived duplicity. Despite her disillusionment, Hailey stayed in the group due to the strong bonds that had formed over time. However, on July 3, 2021, she stirred the pot further by sharing news that Zhang had attended his father's birthday during the BL drama's promotion and was seen with a woman rumored to be his girlfriend. Hailey said,

> I think that since he is a male celebrity who became popular by maifu (making homosexual elements as selling points), the minimum professional conduct is required, right? Isn't it too unprofessional to have the audacity to date his girlfriend while the CP is the promotion?

Penny (a CP-fan) replied, "Don't believe this negative news easily, OK? Maybe it's a rival who deliberately set them both up to divide the CP-fans base." In response, Hailey said, "WAKE UP! Your *ge ge*[3] hugged and wept on stage and then Zhang went home to spend a birthday party with his girlfriend. Can you still get high on such a fake CP?" "Can you be more mature? And do you believe they're actually gay?" Silvia pointedly replied to Hailey, "Doesn't it say something about Zhang's professionalism that he's a straight man and yet he can play BL characters in dramas so vividly?" "That's right, it's enough that he's dedicated enough on stage, it's too much to criticize people's private lives," Rose agreed with Silvia's opinion. CP-fan Wendy suddenly said, "Even though it's true, I still can't like them both anymore, bye," and withdrew from our WeChat group (WeChat group conversation, July 17–18, 2021).

Afterward, we contacted Wendy privately to find out why she had suddenly quit the group, and she cried over the phone:

> Sister, even though I know that CP is mostly fake and marketed, every time I see their heartfelt interactions, I am always still willing to expect if they will have a moment of real love under the surface of acting [...] but now, I don't

---

[3] *ge ge*: "哥哥," The literal meaning of the term is "brother," but within the context of the Chinese language, it serves as an affectionate form of address used by female fans to refer to their male celebrity idols and does not imply any actual familial kinship.

believe in love anymore, all the emotional contribution I've made over the past few months seems to be fed to the dogs! It turns out that all those moments of true love were acted out. Damn Zhang! How dare he look at Gong with that true love in his eyes while having a girlfriend at the same time! He is too "good" at cheating. From today onwards, I don't love either of them anymore, it's all so pointless.

(Wendy, video interview on July 21, 2021)

An uneasy atmosphere pervaded the WeChat group that had lost one member; everyone had their own opinions but were worried that they might influence more fan friends to quit if they spoke too directly. Hailey spoke up again:

Look, it's all Zhang's fault that these hard-earned CP-fans are starting to lose out, so irreverent, he shouldn't have gone down the path of marketing CP to make money from fans. While earning the money CP-fans spend for true love, he boasts that he is a professional actor who should keep his personal life separate from his role. This is being a whore yet claiming to be a chaste woman at the same time.[4]

"Oh," Yumi replied with a sneer, "the more people vilify him, the more I feel sorry for him and the more I love him" (WeChat group conversation, July 20, 2021). Yumi, Rose, and others gradually became Zhang's only-fans, often defending Zhang in the group to the point of frequent quarrels with Hailey and others.

Such tension and antagonism represent a microcosm of what was happening in the broader fan community at the time, with many former CP-fans turning into toxic anti-fans of Zhang and becoming actively involved in the collective

---

[4] "又当婊子又立牌坊" is a Chinese proverb that means to take advantage of both sides.

actions of abusing Zhang by spreading news of his "scandals." Anti-fans posted many photos on Weibo of Zhang and his lady friend together and viciously attacked his private life. It was from Zhang's own CP-fandom that the slur against his political stance first came to light.

Mobilizing Nationalism: Strategies and Victories

Since Zhang's Weibo account was set to only show content from the last six months, the photos he posted before he became famous were only deliberately collected by those who were his original fans, who went to huge efforts to collect his photos from various sources. Such expressions of fan love for their idol later became weapons to ruin him, as some ex-CP-fans discovered a long-hidden photo posted in 2018 from their collections, a set of cherry blossom photos taken during Zhang's trip to Japan. In the background of one photo, a building was recognized as part of the square in front of the Yasukuni Shrine (see Figure 2.3).

Yasukuni Shrine is a place where the Second World War war criminals are enshrined in Japan, and is a place condemned by Chinese people as representing Japanese militarism and a reminder of the Japanese invasion of China. Every year, on the anniversary of Japan's surrender in the Second World War, Japanese politicians visit the Yasukuni Shrine, which is strongly protested and condemned by the Chinese government and is also referred to by the public as *baigui* (worshipping the devil). As a result, Chinese public figures accused of worshipping Yasukuni Shrine are always inevitably strongly criticized by the government and the public.

On the night of August 12, 2021, an anonymous post emerged online with these photos, accusing Zhang of worshipping at the Yasukuni Shrine as a national traitor. During that night and the next day, anti-fans on Weibo

FIGURE 2.3A AND 2.3B *Photos of Zhang in Japan taken in 2018, with one marked to show the alleged "worshipping" at the Yasukuni Shrine.[5] Retrieved from Zhang's Weibo and Douban discussion on September 26, 2021.*

began posting this news in a concerted way, with the same hashtag #*Zhang Zhehan Worshipped in the Yasukuni Shrine*, attempting to drive it up on the rank of trending topics. This scandal exploded like a bomb in fan communities. We found out on the evening of August 12, 2021, when one of our informants in another idol's fandom, Celia, excitedly shared the news with her fan friends. "He's going to be thoroughly cold!" Celia exclaimed, "I finally don't have to see this ugly face on Weibo anymore." "Being cold" is an internet slang in Chinese fandom, which originally means that a person's body turns cold after death, but nowadays has become a metaphor for a celebrity's career being completely ruined.

---

[5]The circles were drawn by an ex-CP-fan, highlighting the building of the Yasukuni Shrine.

The news immediately drew many fans to join the crowd to "eat melon"—another Chinese internet slang—referring to bystanders watching the hilarity, which was explicitly expressed in all WeChat fan groups observed in this study. They excitedly speculated on the extent to which Zhang would be severely punished. Both Celia and these melon-eaters represent the attitude of the general public and other fan communities who expect celebrities to be punished severely, while few care about the justification and legitimacy of such punishment.

At the same time, four only-fans of Zhang finally split from the observed CP-fans WeChat group because they could not stand the quarrels and conflicts with other fans. They created a smaller WeChat group of five (Silvia, Tina, Rose, Yumi, and the first author). The night of August 12 was a long one, and no one in the group slept. Zhang's photos in front of the Yasukuni Shrine began to be circulated widely on social media platforms, and various marketing accounts[6] began to engage in discussions about this trending topic to generate more platform traffic. We witnessed the general public opinion becoming increasingly hostile to Zhang. However, the target of the fans' attention—Zhang himself—was slow to respond to the incident.

We kept an eye on social media platforms like Weibo and Douban, where the discussion was chaotic. Fans who supported Zhang were desperately defending him, explaining that he was only traveling to take photos of cherry blossoms and had unintentionally photographed Yasukuni Shrine. However, negative voices and trolling from anti-fans soon

---

[6]Marketing accounts: in Chinese 营销号, refers to media accounts operated by media institutions, public relations firms, and other organizations on Chinese social media mblatforms. These accounts are responsible for advertising as well as promoting celebrities and media productions. In order to drive higher traffic and attract more followers, these accounts often amplify and disseminate celebrity gossip, as well as sensationalized rumors, by closely aligning their content with trending news.

dominated social media platforms and were joined by other social media users outside of BL and idol fandoms who were angered by the "national traitor."

As mentioned in the introduction, some of our informants became fans of both individual actors, Xiao and Wang, with the popularity of *The Untamed*, another BL-adapted drama. Three of them (Iris, Ole, and Elly) constantly posted negative updates of Zhang with the hashtag *#history does not tolerate ignorance* (#历史不容无视) to heighten public attention, hoping to pressure the government to severely punish Zhang. Meanwhile, they gloated at fan gatherings with the belief that their collective actions would erase a potential rival of their idols and thus contribute to their own idols' career success. We observed and participated in their offline fan discussion in Suzhou about Zhang's incident.

> Zhang is so tragic, he must have been trapped by being too popular in blocking someone's career and having no backers to rely on, right?
>
> (Iris, casual talk at fan gathering,
> Suzhou, September 2, 2021)

> I guess so, with all the ads and endorsements he has received in the six months since he burst onto the scene, when all those business resources were originally for other stars, how could the sponsors behind them [referring to other stars] sit on their hands.
>
> (Elly, casual talk at fan gathering,
> Suzhou, September 2, 2021)

> Great, he had better hurry up to die or my brother will be robbed of all his business resources.
>
> (Iris, casual talk at fan gathering,
> Suzhou, September 2, 2021)

Iris was an only-fan of Wang, the BL star of *The Untamed*, so she deeply believed that Zhang and Gong were a huge threat to Wang. "That's what he deserves! If he didn't have those pictures, his rivals wouldn't be able to harm him," Hailey replied. Notably, Hailey was an only-fan of Gong who actively shared scandals and rumors about Zhang in our CP-fans WeChat group. She was also an only-fan of Xiao. Her multiple fan identities were not uncommon among the fandoms. She was the most active informant in spreading all of Zhang's scandals. When we asked her, "Why do you hate him so much? Well at least he is your *gege*'s [meaning Gong] colleague, right?" she replied:

> Just because they both came from the same drama and became popular at the same time. That's why I hate him so much. All the commercial resources are shared equally. My brother will have everything to himself when Zhang dies! Haha, so lucky.

Their attitude toward Zhang, to a certain degree, demonstrates how rivalries in the Chinese entertainment industry are interpreted in fans' discourses. Fans of BL stars often believe that stars from another BL-adapted drama will become direct competitors to their idols and, therefore, that the sinking of the potential competing star's career, in this case Zhang Zhehan, will give their idols more commercial resources. Thus, apart from the CP-fans' disappointment in the idol due to him being in a heterosexual relationship, there are two other major factors that can generate anti-fans: fans of other BL stars and fans of the "partner" in the CP who also became popular in the same BL drama. This mentality of zero-sum game among BL idol fandoms is intriguing. Some optimistic fan scholars have previously argued that the popularity of BL-adapted dramas raised the visibility of this subculture in the public, which could make homoerotic narratives more widely accepted and contribute to the formation to a stronger counter-public (Hu and Wang 2020). This might lead to the gradual mainstreaming and a bigger market for BL cultural products. However, demonstrated by the fan wars in this case study and our observation, such arguments do not seem to be acknowledged by fans. Instead, fans are usually in panic and regard the rapid increase of BL dramas and their popularity as a crisis. Such reactions could be deeply rooted in the fans' lack of confidence in the mainstreaming of BL themes due to their knowledge about the strong cultural governance of the Party-State and the increasingly stringent censorship regime.

Although these BL dramas provide a swift path to fame for male idols and are a sought-after avenue for companies to create superstars, they remain potential targets of censorship and regulation. Notably, whenever a BL-adapted drama with great popularity and influence emerges, it is often met with demands from the authorities to be taken down from video platforms (e.g., *Guardian* and *The Untamed*). Consequently, fans' affection for BL culture is frequently tinged with a complex sense of despair: "When *The Word of Honor* was airing, it was so exciting. We eagerly waited for the release of each episode, fearing that the drama might be banned tomorrow" (Rose, casual conversation in WeChat group, May 13, 2021).

Pervasive censorship has become an ever-present specter, permeating the entire BL culture. BL-adapted dramas have become a gamble for capital, platforms, and fans, all hoping that such products work and the involved male idols can reach sufficient fame before the sword of censorship descends. The struggle unfolds constantly between the profit-driven entertainment market and the ideology-based cultural governance of the Party-State. As anticipated by the informants, BL-adapted drama *The Word of Honor* was indeed banned in August 2021, and the National Radio Television Administration (NRTA) even introduced stricter policies in January 2022, resulting in the cancellation of all planned BL-adapted dramas (ChinaNews 2022).[7] To date (September 2023), not a single BL-adapted drama has aired in full since *The Word of Honor*. Even in cases where BL dramas are successfully aired, the dramas and involved idols are under constant scrutiny of competing agencies and fandoms. Competitors can and usually manage to find faults in the content, the leading actors, marketing strategies, and social impact of these dramas, as reasons to report the drama to the supervising government department.

Their uncertainties and perceived risks cause apprehension and panic among fans, making them prone to taking more aggressive actions to maximize their idols' benefit as soon as possible. However, paradoxically, these aggressive actions reinforce the public perception of BL culture as harmful, illegitimate, and unacceptable, which fails to generate support for the homoerotic subculture and challenge the dominance of heteronormative narratives in the Chinese pop cultural industries. Therefore, for every male idol who attains fame through a BL drama, the subsequent step is to distance themselves from the "BL" and "homosexuality" labels and reshape their mainstream image to gain public acceptance and avoid potential censorship. This path back to the mainstream is not without challenges, competition, and risks, which usually come from rival agencies and fandoms. Fans, therefore, find themselves in an extremely sensitive and aggressive state and in need of combating any potential rivals that might threaten their idols. Gradually, a vicious cycle of insecurity-aggression-marginalization forms, and BL fans embrace the discourses of zero-sum game and defending idols from rivals' attacks. Demonstrated in this primer's case study, Zhang's fans believe that Zhang's scandal is a result of the rivals' framing.

---

[7]https://www.chinanews.com.cn/yl/2022/01-07/9646380.shtml (Retrieved July 29, 2023).

Canceled: The Consequences of Nationalist Fan Mobilization

On the morning of August 13, Zhang posted an open letter of apology on his Weibo account (see Figure 2.4). He explained that he had accidentally captured the Yasukuni Shrine building in a photograph taken during a trip to Japan and did not

FIGURE 2.4 *Apology posted by Zhang on Weibo in the morning of August 13. Retrieved August 13, 2021. Zhang's Weibo account is now banned.*

enter the shrine to worship. He also emphasized, "I cannot accept the accusations against my political stance. I have always been a patriotic person." Following Zhang's apology, the state-run media *People's Daily* posted a commentary on Weibo, criticizing Zhang that "as a public figure, he should not have such a lack of common sense about history" (see Figure 2.5). Interestingly, since *People's Daily*'s criticism did not fully align with anti-fans' narrative and only vaguely called for boycotting Zhang, a large number of social media users questioned the paper's political stance and called for the authorities to officially ban Zhang in the comments on this post. The overwhelming outrage and demands from the public on social media platforms soon pressured the authorities and state-owned media outlets to issue harsher condemnation against Zhang.

Meanwhile, Japanese Defense Minister Kishi Nobuo's visit to the Yasukuni Shrine on August 13 immediately became the hottest topic on Weibo, prompting harsh criticism and anger on Chinese social media, which were later shifted toward Zhang. In the comments under the official media's posts condemning Kishi Nobuo, users mentioned that Zhang also worshipped in the Yasukuni Shrine, demanded the banning of Zhang, named Zhang as a national traitor who should get out of China, and even cursed his family. So later on August 14, Zhang's and his agency's accounts on various Chinese social media platforms were totally banned. All his endorsement brands terminated the contracts. While there was no official investigation or announcement from the authorities, Chinese social media users were convinced that these occurrences were evidence that could convict Zhang, which legitimized their boycotting.

By August 15, with the seventy-sixth anniversary of Japan's surrender in the Second World War approaching, Zhang's cancellation reached an even greater crescendo. The cancellation of Zhang was made official in an announcement by the Chinese Performing Arts Association (CAPA). CAPA stated that national histories and relevant knowledge should be common sense

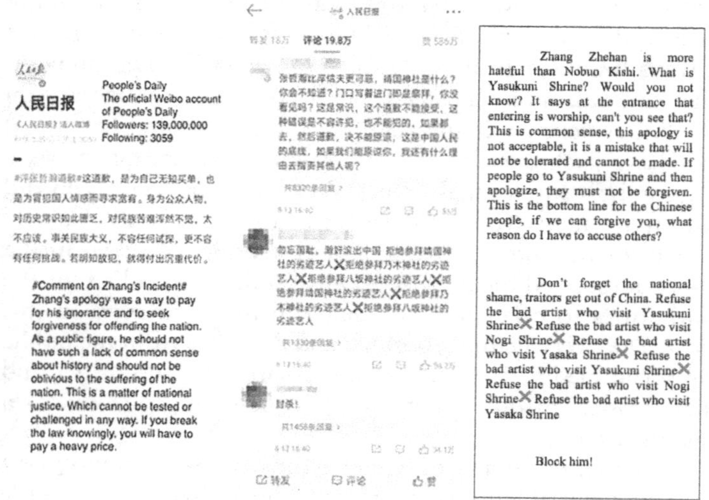

FIGURE 2.5A–C People's Daily's *commentary on Zhang's incident and the three most liked users' comments. Retrieved from Weibo on September 26, 2021.*

for Chinese celebrities, so ignorance cannot excuse Zhang's misconduct. This announcement further stressed that Zhang's highly improper behavior not only harms the nation, but also brings bad influence on youths who follow him as an idol. At the same time, the Central Commission for Discipline Inspection (CCDI) also released a sternly worded commentary, "history does not tolerate ignorance," and that such a celebrity must be boycotted. "China is firmly opposed to all 'devil worship,' if our domestic public figures are not condemned and held accountable for going to the Yasukuni Shrine, how can we stand up straight and ask foreigners not to go?" Soon, the hashtag *#CCDI-comment-on-Zhang's-incident* reached the top of Weibo's hot topic rank.

FIGURE 2.6A AND 2.6B *Search results of Zhang on Bilibili.com. Retrieved from Bilibili.com on September 26, 2021.*

In the following days, the cancellation reached another level as more state media and organizations commented on Zhang's incident. August 16 saw the banning of Zhang's Baidu BBS; August 21 saw the web drama *The Word of Honor* starring Zhang being removed from the video website; and August 23 saw the removal of all fan-made videos from the search results of Zhang by the video-sharing site Bilibili, leaving only the videos from official media that condemned Zhang's behavior (Figure 2.6).

FIGURE 2.7 *The online video version of the film* 1921 *replaces Zhang with another actor. Retrieved on September 25, 2021 (1921 directed by Huang Jianxin and Zheng Dasheng © Tencent Pictures, Shanghai Film Group Co. Ltd., Dimension Films Co., Ltd., China Literature Limited. All rights reserved).*

Immediately afterward, Zhang's name was found to be silently removed from the charity thank-you letter for his previous donation of 1 million yuan to support the flooding in Henan Province. On September 2, the Chinese General Administration of Radio, Film and Television and the Ministry of Propaganda issued an initiative stating that artists and celebrities with bad records need to be boycotted by the entire industry and cannot be defended. On September 25, the film *1921* was released on online video platforms with another actor's footage replacing Zhang's original acting of the same character (see Figure 2.7). The specific process of each step of canceling has been included in Table 1.

After learning about this intense cancellation case, you might wonder: how to understand such cancellation? On the one hand, it shows traits of participation and social movement. On the other hand, it shows traits of censorship. In the following chapter, we will provide a concept that helps you understand such a paradoxical phenomenon and walk you through our analysis of (anti)fan practices in Zhang's case.

TABLE 1 Steps in Zhang's boycott by media platforms and the authorities

Date	Who was involved	What they did
August 13, 2021	Weibo account of *CCTV News*.	Commented that "artists must know their honor and shame, and as Chinese people should remember history."
August 13, 2021	Weibo account of *Thought Torch*, the official account of the Research Centre for National Cultural Security and Ideological Construction at Chinese Academy of Social Sciences.	Questioned the veracity of Zhang's claim of ignorance in his apology, deliberately suggesting that it was not a coincidence, which earned much support from nationalist social media users.
August 13, 2021	Japanese Defense Minister Kishi Nobuo visited the Yasukuni Shrine, which immediately became the hottest topic on Weibo.	Prompted harsh criticism from citizens and shifted this anger onto Zhang. In the comments of the Weibo news condemning Kishi Nobuo, social media users mentioned that Zhang also worshiped at the Yasukuni Shrine and demanded that he be banned, called on the traitor to get out of China, and even cursed his family: "When to punish the national traitor Zhang?" "Devil worshipper, get out of China!" "Is Zhang's mother a Japanese spy? Please investigate."

Date	Who was involved	What they did
August 14, 2021	In a since-deleted Weibo post, Zhan An (斩鞍), a popular novelist, reposted Zhang's news from *China Comment*, a magazine often seen as one of the Party's official mouthpieces.	Zhan An commented, "So I can't even visit the Yasukuni Shrine? It's inexplicable." Facing a swift backlash, Zhan An was forced to offer a lengthy explanation within an hour, suggesting that "the purpose of a visit should be to better understand Japan's national character and history." His account was banned by Weibo. *China Comment* posted a screenshot of Zhan An's original post with a resolute assertion: "No, never!" Zhan An was removed from the production of the TV adaptation of his book.
August 14, 2021	Weibo platform, followed by other platforms.	Zhang's and his studio's accounts were totally banned by Weibo; this was followed by similar actions by other media platforms.
August 15, 2021 (the 76th anniversary of Japan's surrender in the Second World War)	The Chinese Performing Arts Association (CAPA) on Weibo.	CAPA said "it is a common sense for celebrities to know the history, and ignorance is not an excuse." It added that "the Yasukuni Shrine is the symbol of Japanese militarism in launching its invasion war and a place where right-wing Japanese deny the history and beautify the war." "Zhang's highly improper behavior not only harms the nation but also brings bad influence on youths who follow him as an idol." As a result, CAPA reprimanded Zhang and urged a boycott of Zhang in the industry.

Date	Who was involved	What they did
August 15, 2021	Weibo account of the Central Commission for Discipline Inspection (CCDI), the highest disciplinary organ of the Communist Party of China. Its comments were interpreted by social media users as the central government's attitude to this incident.	Released a sternly worded commentary saying that "history does not tolerate ignorance and such a star must be boycotted" … "China is firmly opposed to all 'devil worship,' if our domestic public figures are not condemned and held accountable for going to the Yasukuni Shrine, how can we stand up straight and ask foreigners not to go?" Meanwhile, the hashtag *#CCDI comment on Zhang's incident* reached the top of Weibo's trending topics.
August 16, 2021	Zhang's Baidu Tieba (a forum-like platform).	Zhang's Baidu BBS was banned by Baidu.
August 21, 2021	Youku.com, the video website producing *The Word of Honor.*	The web drama *The Word of Honor* was removed from Youku.com
August 23, 2021	Bilibili.com, the video-sharing website	All fan-made videos from the search results of Zhang were blocked, leaving only the videos from official media condemning Zhang's behavior.
September 2, 2021	National Radio Television Administration (NRTA) and the Ministry of Propaganda	Issued an initiative stating that "the artists with bad records and incorrect political stance need to be boycotted from the entire network and cannot be defended references."

Date	Who was involved	What they did
September 25, 2021	The film *1921*, in which Zhang had starred.	The film was released on online video platforms, with another actor replacing Zhang's role and the film using additional shots instead of Zhang's footage.

CHAPTER THREE

Nationalist Fandom Practices as Participatory Censorship

Zhang's incident might remind you of the trendy yet controversial phenomenon—cancel culture. And indeed, what we can observe in Zhang's disappearance from the Chinese media landscape demonstrates how the public can be mobilized to withdraw various forms of support and investment due to a celebrity's misconduct or problematic speech (Ng 2022). As previous researchers point out, cancellation is not something completely new. Public shaming, boycotting, or blacklisting in the name of social justice are all precedents of cancel culture (Clark 2020; Trottier et al. 2024). The controversies of cancel culture in the public and sometimes also in academia normally lie in its legitimacy, efficacy, and consequences (Bouvier 2020; Norris 2023). Some critics and citizens are concerned about the mob mentality, the lack of due process, and the potential chilling effect or infringement of freedom of speech (Norris 2023). Meanwhile, supporters of this practice emphasize its function of holding powerful individuals accountable when the system is too broken and power relations are too unbalanced, especially for marginalized communities (Clark 2020).

These discussions also take place in China. It seems that cancel culture is universal globally. However, we need to recognize that due to different sociopolitical contexts, Chinese cases need extra care when being discussed as another illustration of the globalized cancel culture. Specifically, the actors and the power relations involved in these procedures need to be contextualized, revealed, and discussed. Chinese fan cultures interact much more closely with the state power than its Western counterpart (Jenkins 2020), and the state power permeates the Chinese society not only in an incidental but a structural and fundamental manner (Huang et al. 2023). Therefore, in this chapter, we will dive into some relevant practices normalized in Chinese idol fandoms, explain how they can be understood as participatory censorship, and then illustrate how such participatory censorship was conducted in Zhang's incident.

The Normalized Fandom Practice: Accusatory Reporting, with Guidebooks!

Before we explain how Chinese fans and citizens collectively cancel idols in fan wars, some technical and political conditions that enable such mass accusatory reporting need to be explained in detail. The Party-State has strong intentions and immense capability to control public opinions and the media landscape in general (Fang and Repnikova 2018). Yet, the internet has developed so fast that the government does not have sufficient capacity to oversee every information exchange on every platform, so the Party-State delegates the responsibility of surveillance and censorship to all the social media platforms (Ye et al. 2023).

Taking Weibo, one of the most important and popular platforms for Chinese fans, as an example, every account has to be registered under a real name and mobile number that can only be acquired when ID or passport is presented. By doing so, every account is traceable. In addition, Weibo introduced reporting features that allow individual users to report other users' accounts, posts, or comments. These reports will be transferred to the platform's administrators to determine whether these reports are valid and whether the reported users should be punished in the form of a temporary or permanent ban. When reporting, users can choose from a list of reasons that are divided into eleven main categories, with more specific reasons in each category. For example, as shown in Figure 3.1, if a user chooses "harmful information" as the main category for reporting, they then need to choose from the following specific reasons: cults, insulting martyrs, terrorism, historical nihilism, religious and ethnic issues, animal cruelty, and other harmful information. While these

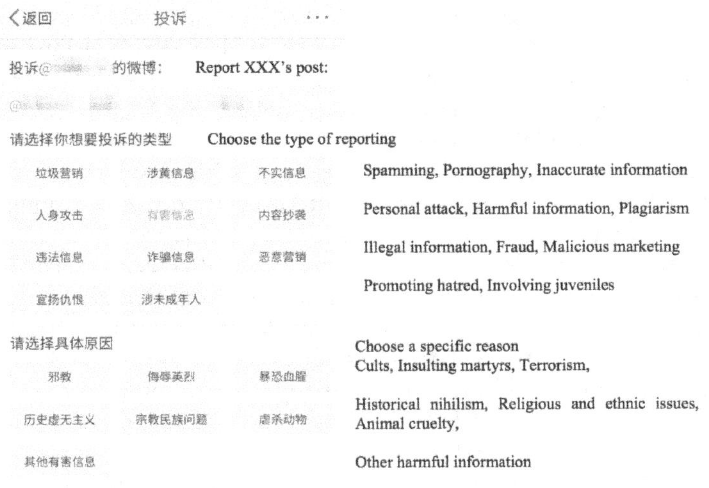

〈返回　　　　　　投诉　　　　　　　　　· · ·

投诉@ ▨▨ 的微博:　　　Report XXX's post:

@ ▨▨

请选择你想要投诉的类型　　　Choose the type of reporting

垃圾营销	涉黄信息	不实信息	Spamming, Pornography, Inaccurate information
人身攻击	有害信息	内容抄袭	Personal attack, Harmful information, Plagiarism
违法信息	诈骗信息	恶意营销	Illegal information, Fraud, Malicious marketing
宣扬仇恨	涉未成年人		Promoting hatred, Involving juveniles

请选择具体原因　　　Choose a specific reason

邪教	侮辱英烈	暴恐血腥	Cults, Insulting martyrs, Terrorism,
历史虚无主义	宗教民族问题	虐杀动物	Historical nihilism, Religious and ethnic issues, Animal cruelty,
其他有害信息			Other harmful information

FIGURE 3.1 *The Weibo reporting interface. Captured by the first author on November 23, 2022.*

categories and reasons are clarified, it was never clear what and how certain content would be censored or lead to account banning (Wang and Tan 2023). The censorship mechanisms are essentially imaginaries perceived by the fans who engage with the reporting practices day in and day out.

Under such circumstances, fans share their experience and knowledge within their fandom community to identify effective ways to make use of censorship to defend their and their idols' interests. To win a conflict or a fan war, sub-fandom communities strategically work with these reporting mechanisms on the platforms. In fan wars, fans often pool their individual experiences and construct a "reporting guidebook" to successfully defeat rival fans by getting them banned by platforms or even punished by authorities. In these guidebooks, fans can find tactics that are tested by their fellow fans and proven to be effective. These guidebooks are normally distributed by lead fans who have more amplification capacity due to their large number of followers and then circulated widely within the fan community to guide individual fans in their collective accusatory reporting to win the fan war. Details, examples, and comparisons are provided. For example, one informant explains: "you should accuse an enemy of 'an anti-communist stance,' as it may be dealt with more efficiently by platform administrators than if you accuse your enemy of 'obscene pornography'" (Hailey, in-person interview, Suzhou, May 2021). By doing so, the enemy might also receive harsher penalties from both the platform and law enforcement, such as a full deletion of their social media account and relevant real-life punishment. Usually, such practices aim to "kill the enemies in one blow." In our digital ethnography, we gain access to some of such "reporting guidebooks," one of which is shown in Figure 3.2.

Following these guidebooks, fans regularly participate in and carry out collective accusatory reporting activities. For some fans, it even becomes a daily task and an obligation

[rsgj]该博主用低俗的语言恶意骚扰并攻击本人，其暴力低俗言论严重危害了网友和本人的身心健康，造成了极其恶劣的影响，同时该微博用户的行为也严重违反了《微博社区管理规定》，严重破坏网络治安环境，已构成网络社会公害，不符合"清朗行动"整治饭圈乱象的目的，请严肃处理，谢谢！[人身gjw]

[恶意yx]通过造谣明星、蹭热点等方式。其微博中有大量的引战内容，发布明星内容引起粉丝互撕谩骂、拉踩引战、造谣攻击。追星应当理性文明，适度有节，而不是通过微博的流量制造"引战"话题等各种干扰正常网络信息传播秩序，危害社区良性生态的行为。正值国家"清朗行动"期间，希望平台可以快速处理 [引z]

[恶意yx]此人言论属于造谣，严重危害了艺人明星的名誉权。同时该用户的暴力低俗言论严重危害未成年网友身心健康，严重违反了《微博社区管理规定(试行)》，严重破坏网络治安环境。请尽快处理，谢谢。[引z]

[恶意yx]此用户发布的微博有诱导未成年人无底线追星、互撕谩骂等导向不良的行为，为获取流量和利益，随意造谣误导公众，使用侮辱性、低俗性词汇人身攻击明星本人，存在恶意营销行为。其行为已违反《微博社区公约》，严重侵害个人合法权益，影响微博社区网络环境以及微博使用观感。请严肃处理，谢谢！[引z]

【yhxx】该微博用及其下流的语言侮辱、恶意谩骂公众人物，对该公众人物造成了恶劣影响，严重侵犯了演员的名誉权。该用户的暴力低俗言论严重危害未成年网友身心健康，严重违反了《微博社区管理规定(试行)》，严重破坏网络治安环境，已构成网络社会公害。请尽快严肃处理，谢谢其他[yhxx]

[Personal Attack] The blogger used vulgar language to maliciously harass and attack me, and his/her violent and vulgar comments **seriously endangered** the physical and mental health of netizens and myself, causing an **extremely bad impact**, while the blogger's behaviour also **seriously violated** the "**Weibo Community Management Regulations**" and **seriously damaged** the online security environment, which has constituted an online social nuisance and **is not in line with the "Sweep-up Campaign",** Please deal with this **seriously**. [Personal attack on me]

[Malicious Marketing] By disinforming celebrities and rubbing hot spots. There is a lot of content in their posts leading to fan war, posting star content causing fans to abuse each other, triggering fan wars and rumourmongering to attack each other. It is important to be rational and civilised and to exercise moderation in loving stars, rather than using the traffic data of Weibo to create war-topics that **interfere with the normal order of online information dissemination and endanger the healthy ecology of society.** I hope that this will be dealt with **quickly** during the national "**Sweep-up Campaign**". [Leading a war].

[Malicious Marketing] This person's comments are disinformation and **seriously** jeopardize the star's **right to reputation**. At the same time the user's violent and vulgar comments **seriously** endangered the physical and mental health **of underage netizens, seriously** violated the **Weibo Community Management Regulations** (for Trial Implementation), and **seriously** damaged the online security environment. Please deal with this as soon as possible, thank you. [Leading a war]

[Malicious Marketing] This person released a post which has **induced underage to the bottomless idolisation,** abusing each other, and other **badly oriented behaviour,** to obtain traffic data and interests, randomly create rumours **to mislead the public,** use insulting, vulgar words to personally attack the stars themselves. There is malicious marketing behaviour. Their behaviour has violated the **"Weibo Community Convention", seriously** infringed on **the legitimate rights and interests** of individuals and **affected the network environment** of the Weibo community and **the perception of Weibo usage.** Please deal with them **seriously**, thank you! [Leading a War]

[Harmful Information] This post uses **extremely** nasty language to insult and maliciously abuse a **public figure,** causing a bad impact on that public figure and **seriously** violating their **right to reputation.** The user has **seriously** endangered the physical and mental health of **underage netizens** with violent and vulgar comments, **seriously** violated the "Weibo Community Management Regulations (for Trial Implementation)", **seriously** damaged **the online security environment,** and has constituted an online social nuisance. Please deal with it **seriously** as soon as possible, thank you! [Other harmful information]

FIGURE 3.2A AND 3.2B *Reporting guidebook, posted by a big fan and circulated in an idol's only-fan community on Weibo. Captured on Weibo and annotated by the first author on December 23, 2022.*

that proves their fan identities and earns them entry to the fan community. For instance, one of the criteria for checking a fan's loyalty is to see if they have "punched in" for "battling anti-fans missions":

Battling anti-fans becomes our daily task. Every day, the battling anti-fans team[1] posts a reporting task on its Weibo account, with links to the posts that need to be reported and the reporting guidebook telling us which reason to choose. [After completing the task], we leave comments under this post to declare that I have completed the task. It is like "punch-in" [at work].
(Silvia, video interview, WeChat, March 27, 2021)

When some fans have disputes within their fandom community and their loyalty is questioned, they often post screenshots of these "punch-ins" to prove their dedication to their idols. These participating fans often do not verify whether the subject of the report is indeed "illegal," but they engage in accusatory reporting as their daily tasks. Thus, the act of accusatory reporting is routinized and legitimized as a daily fan participation that can prove someone's fan identity.

Such collective accusatory reporting is common among fandoms of BL-adapted dramas and involved idol actors. Before the focal case study—Zhang's incident—took place, several other high-profile incidents grasped not only the attention of fandom communities but also the general public in China. One of such incidents is "The 227 Incident," where the collective accusatory reporting from a sub-fandom (only-fans of Xiao, one of the leading actors) led to an important cultural

---

[1]The battling anti-fans team, literally "anti-black team," 反黑组, refers to a subdivision within online fan communities that is responsible for mobilizing members to collectively report social media posts and rumor threads perceived as detrimental to their idol (Wang and Ge 2023).

product for another sub-fandom (CP-fans of Xiao and Wang) censored by the Chinese Party-State (Huang et al. 2023; Wang and Ge 2023). Due to the overlaps between BL-adapted drama fan communities, many of our informants were also engaged in the fandom of the drama involved in "The 227 Incident": *The Untamed*, which allows us to also collect supporting data to understand the background and community cultures where Zhang's incident later developed. Without diving too deep into "The 227 Incident" itself to avoid derailing from our main case study, we would like to show some examples from their guidebooks and their accusatory reporting practices to provide you with empirical material before we continue our conceptualization in the next section.

On February 14, 2020, a CP-fan author published her fan fiction about the couple on Weibo, Lofter (www.lofter. com), and Archive of Our Own (www.archiveofourown.org, thereafter AO3)[2] simultaneously. This fiction titled *Xiazhui* (*Falling*) is an erotic story between Xiao, who is imagined as a transgender prostitute, and Wang, who is figured as a high school student. Such a controversial theme was then detected by Xiao's only-fans, giving rise to their strongly expressed dissatisfaction with this erotic writing and later their collective accusatory reporting on this fan fiction to the Weibo content moderation team, Lofter, and CAC, claiming the fiction's explicit erotic descriptions of illegal prostitution could have an extremely detrimental influence on juveniles. They did so under the guidance of crowdsourced guidebooks circulated within their fandom. For instance, a post on February 26, 2020 by an influential only-fan with over 100,000 followers on Weibo guided other only-fans to contact the CAC by arguing that the dissemination of the fiction would cause mental health problems and introduce unhealthy values to underage internet

---

[2]Lofter is a Chinese website for sharing fiction or illustrations, and AO3 is its international counterpart, both of which are used widely by fans to create, share, and discuss fan-made works.

users. The post also emphasized that phone calls to CAC would be the most effective way for such reporting. As Hailey highlighted in the interview above, the core purpose of fans' collective accusatory reporting is to get the person punished as quickly as possible, so fans tend to exaggerate the accusations to ensure "the reported cases are dealt with more quickly, the more people report them, the faster they are dealt with."

As a result, these guidebooks show patterns that fit such purposes. Firstly, templates and suggestions for accusatory reporting are intentionally diversified and segmented even in the same main category to ensure more targeted effectiveness. For example, under the category of "malicious marketing," different content will highlight different kinds of negative impact. The selection of a suitable reason template is often the result of lead fans' thoughtful analysis. Secondly, these reporting templates push for more serious accusations when describing the negative impact. This includes the explicit wording of "seriously" and "extremely"—even though this description is often overstated for the purposes of reporting. Thirdly, these templates tend to highlight the potential harmful impact on underage social media users to add another layer of urgency and significance for the authorities to deal with accused content or accounts. Finally, all templates explicitly point out that the accused matter violates Weibo's regulations and guidelines in the critical period of the government's Sweep-up Campaign, with the belief that this will urge Weibo's content moderators to deal with the accusatory report as soon as possible.

These tactics and guidebooks seem to be effective as the fan communities continue to operate in this way. Meanwhile, an interesting development of CAC's Sweep-up Campaign series took place in July 2020, where CAC announced that it would "pay close attention to fans' blind idolization of celebrities and the prevalence of fan conflicts." It is hard not to connect such development to the social impact brought by high-profile cases such as "The 227 Incident." And it is also ironic that aligning with and using CAC's discourses does not grant fans immunity in this campaign series.

Conceptualize Participatory Censorship

When we look at the fans' collective accusatory reporting practices, we can see two elements that might seem contradictory to each other: participation and censorship. In fandom studies literature, these two phenomena are usually pitted against each other. Since Jenkins (2009) proposes the concept of participatory culture to highlight fans' active and voluntary participation enabled by the internet that fundamentally differs from the traditional audiences' passive media consumption, researchers across cultural contexts provide various empirically informed discussions about the significance and limitation of fans' participation. These discussions range across the democratization capacity of fan activism (Zhou and Miao 2019; Liao et al. 2022), the potential to form counter-publics based on fandom objects (Hu and Wang 2021), and the fan labor involved in these processes (e.g., Stanfill 2019, 2020; Yin 2020; Zhang and Negus 2020). In China specifically, there has been a large body of fandom research spotlighting how fans' participation can circumvent censorship though practices such as crowdsourcing information about censorship mechanism and co-producing creative expressions (e.g., Yang and Xu 2016; Hu and Wang 2021; Hu et al. 2024b). The fandom studies and, specifically, research about participatory culture, therefore, cannot escape from investigating tensions between mainstream and marginalized cultures and communities, as well as hegemonic power and resistance.

The phenomenon of censorship is an ultimate demonstration of these tensions and the power relations in pop cultural industries. Broadly speaking, censorship should be understood as a heterogeneous process, realized through the relationships between censorious agents, of structurally inhibiting or prohibiting dissemination of ideas, information, images, and other messages through communication channels (Jansen 1988; Freshwater 2004). This understanding differs from the more commonly accepted narrow definition of censorship, which only refers to the state apparatus'— especially ones of authoritarian regimes—repression of speech through suppressing, deleting, and controlling content deemed objectionable (Richter 2008; Sun and Zhao 2022). Researchers also differentiate between different types of censorship based on the censorious agents, such as state censorship, self-censorship, and delegated censorship (Sun and Zhao 2022). However, what if the censorious agents are civilians and common social media users, just as in the debates about cancel culture and relevant cases like Zhang's incident? What if the inhibition and prohibition of a cultural product's dissemination is achieved through participation?

Here, we would like to introduce and further develop a conceptual framework to analyze this phenomenon: participatory censorship. Several Chinese researchers have endeavored to establish this concept, and each of their conceptualizations brings out different focal points. Luo and Li (2022) studied the Chinese online *danmei* community to understand how fans navigate the unknown censorship on social media platforms and how they adjust their behaviors. By doing so, they point out that the uncertainty brought by the opaque censorship mechanisms in China makes users speculate and imagine how censorship works and thus engage in activities that take advantage of such censorship and state power, such as accusatory reporting, to achieve their goals (ibid.). Their conceptualization of participatory censorship highlights the paradoxical dynamic where censorship "relies on the voluntary participation of actors who are simultaneously subject to being censors" (p. 4). Similar to Luo and Li, Wang and Tan (2023) also examine fan activities in Chinese BL fandom to argue that, afforded by designs and policies of digital platforms, these fans actively participate in decentralized censorship, which should be understood as participatory censorship. Wang and Tan's empirical analysis dives deeper into the specific participatory censorious activities in Chinese BL fandoms, such as accusatory reporting, account targeting, comment controlling, and blacklisting, and relevant technical features and political economy of involved digital platforms (ibid.). Built upon a different type of empirical case study, the gameplay of *Animal Crossing: New Horizons*, Song (2023) conceptualizes participatory censorship as "the community-based self-censorship practice that seeks to depoliticize gameplay and pledge allegiance with the authorities" (p. 1454). Different from the previous two conceptualizations, Song focuses on active self-censorship practices, especially depoliticizing the gameplay and the expressions of regime-supporting popular nationalism, rather than the decentralized censorious practices carried out by fans against other individuals. Despite some differences in conceptualizing participatory censorship, all authors touch upon the voluntary nature, fans' active participation, outcomes of suppressed or moderated speech or cultural product, and the sociopolitical environment with undeniable state power that fosters surveillance and censorship in many forms. All of them also explicitly articulate the need to break away from the simplified understanding of censorship as a pure top-down process that takes place only in authoritarian countries.

Informed by the observed fandom practices during the fieldwork—especially the accusatory reporting guidebooks—and building on these three insightful conceptualization articles as well as previous literature on cancel culture, participatory culture, and censorship, we would like to propose a comprehensive conceptual framework of participatory censorship to understand the phenomena that often get conflated as cancel culture and toxic fan practices such as getting celebrities banned and silencing anti-fans or rival fans. We define participatory censorship as: individuals who are not political agents (individuals or communities) who voluntarily engage in participatory practices with the intention of controlling discourses, information flows, and/or the development of (fandom) incidents while aligning with the interests, narrative, values, and norms of power holders.

Let's break down and dive into the important elements in this definition.

Voluntary engagement of non-political individuals (subjects): To qualify as participatory actions, the subjects of such actions need to be agents who do not function as or on behalf of political institutions. Based on relevant definitions in political science (Quick and Bryson 2022) and fandom studies (Jenkins 2006, 2009), which our conceptualization builds upon, the participatory nature of actions comes from the subjects' civilian identities and the low threshold to take actions. However, it is important to note that the non-political-agent identity and the voluntariness of their engagement do not mean that these actors and actions are free from political influence. Participatory practices (means) include the consuming and (re)producing of relevant cultural products (e.g., purchasing concert tickets and merchandise, making fan art, posting, and commenting), organizing collective actions, as well as (the appeal to) the withdrawal of the above-mentioned.

Intention to control (ends): In addition to the conventional intentions of censorship, including controlling discourses, information flows, and ideologies, fans' intentions to participate in censorial practices are complicated by the desire to control the development of (fandom) incidents (e.g., increase/decrease idols' popularity, the resolution of idols'/fans' conflicts, resolution of perceived idols'/fans' perceived offences). This will also be further explored in Chapter 4, where we shift our attention to how business interests come to play.

Aligning with power holders (power relation): Embedded power imbalance is essential in defining censorship as it usually relies on the overwhelming cultural/political/ economic powers to repress expressions. Such power relations will not be cancelled out by the participatory and voluntary nature of the censorial actions as long as the participants align themselves with the power holders' interests, narrative, values, and norms.

Hereby, we provide a clear definition of participatory censorship by integrating previous scholarships that coined and informed this term. This conceptual framework also re-emphasizes and formalizes key analytical angles of studying diverse global expressions of cancel culture: subjects, means, ends, and power relations.

We also want to emphasize that such participatory censorship can also escalate to online violence and potentially transcend the digital realm. We now demonstrate these tragic consequences with our informant Yumi's experience. We chose to spotlight her experience because her case generated a considerable amount of public discussion at the time it occurred. We have also intentionally obscured information about Yumi's true identity, occupation, and geographic location to avoid her being identified by other members of her fan community and, in particular, by the fans who reported her.

Yumi was a fan informant we interviewed in depth during my fieldwork in Y city in 2021, and we had previously become good friends in the same WeChat fan group, participating in discussions about the fantasy of male celebrities coupling. We were introduced to Yumi by another informant, Rose, and had the opportunity to meet her when we visited Y city. At the time, we probably would not have invited Yumi to be one of my informants had it not been for such an incident that happened to her. She just seemed like a very common CP-fan, firmly believing that there was a genuine love between male stars A and B, and writing a lot of fan BL novels about them. However, one day in 2021, male star A was reported by his anti-fans en masse and banned by the state authorities after he did something that was deemed unacceptable. Yumi defended

A on Weibo when this incident unfolded, so she also became an accusatory reporting target of many angry anti-fans.

As we scouted for an appropriate interview venue in the bustling streets of Y city, her demeanor took on a hint of embarrassment as she suggested, "Could we choose a more budget-friendly location? I'm facing financial constraints at the moment." Once we reassured her of our intent to cover the expenses, a visible sense of relief washed over her countenance. She explained to us, "It is related to 'that incident.' The company reassigned me to the library as a librarian, which means a reduced income compared to my previous role."[3] "That incident" refers to the cancellation of star A and the targeting of Yumi. When A was accused by his anti-fans of violating public morality, Weibo immediately banned A's account. Meanwhile, Yumi, a CP-fan of A, posted several comments on Weibo to defend A's plight during the ban. Not only did the anti-fans accuse A of unacceptable behavior in the past, but they also "patrolled the square" to seek potential targets among A's fans. Unfortunately, Yumi was one of these targets. A's anti-fans took screenshots of Yumi's posts in defense of A and sent them to some marketing accounts, where they became a talking point, prompting a wave of ridicule of Yumi and other A's fans for being "brain-dead fans" who "idolize A without bottom-line." This narrative was incorporated by official media outlets in their commentaries and the later Sweep-up campaign. As these screenshots did not hide Yumi's Weibo account handle, Yumi was unfortunately doxed by vigilantes, with her personal information, such as real name, company, and occupation exposed. More severely, these vigilantes reported her screenshots to her company, accusing her of unacceptable behaviors and questioning her

---

[3]Please note that we have changed Yumi's occupation for confidentiality purposes.

work ethics and abilities. During that period, the hashtag of Yumi's name was even featured in the trending topic ranks on Weibo. Then, Weibo banned Yumi's account as a response to the boiling debates.

> It's inconsequential; Weibo's intent is to quell the uproar. Muting me and making me vanish is one of their most effective strategies. The people who reported these screenshots to my company are rabid anti-fans of A, extremely hateful of A, and consequently angry at every ordinary fan who defends A. I merely had the misfortune of being a demonstration for them to make an example out of. I was the one who was careless enough to reveal my physical identity on social media.
>
> (Yumi, in-person interview, Y city, certain time)

When queried about the origin of her exposure, Yumi disclosed,

> Two years ago, I had posted some complaints at work and brought up my company's location. That's how they found my company and my real name. Because some of my fan friends betrayed me.
>
> (Yumi, in-person interview, Y city, certain time)

She recounted her transition from a prior fan community, where she formed close fan friends who knew her real identity, to embracing a new CP fandom—star A slash B. However, this transition caused her friendships to unravel. Consequently, her real identity and other personal information became a hostage, "These supporting-A posts of mine irritated them, and they were even too willing to join forces with the extremist fandom police, exposing my identity."

The repercussions extended beyond the digital realm, as Yumi's company's Weibo account weathered attacks and interrogation regarding the handling of an employee with "problematic values." Consequently, the company issued a public statement on Weibo outlining its approach to managing the situation, eventually leading to Yumi's removal from her position. Yumi offered a sardonic perspective, underscoring the gravity of her circumstance:

> But luckily, I didn't say anything illegal, and they had to report it to my company in the hope that I would be punished. Otherwise, the person who posted the written announcement on Weibo might not be my company, but Peace Y City (the Weibo account of Y city's Police).
>
> (Yumi, in-person interview, Y city, certain time)

The interview concluded on a solemn note, Yumi cautioning, "My dear, you should also be careful never to reveal your identity on your fan's social media accounts." Because for fans, who usually have more than one social media account, they often have a dedicated account for one fan community and a new account for another idol to avoid their fan friends seeing information that is not relevant to their idol—the person can never predict whether their fan friend will be an anti-fan of another idol and take offense at them for it. This has actually become a common means of self-censorship for fans, just as Yumi has repeatedly expressed regret that she revealed her true information on her account. Fans have resorted to these self-censorship measures in order to avoid having themselves reported and compromising their identity in real life.

As we can see through Yumi's unfortunate ordeal, the consequences of participatory censorship extend to real life, threatening the security and well-being of individual fans physically and financially. Its success also reveals the uncertainty of the Chinese state's censorship mechanism and the opaqueness of internet governance in China, which are in place mainly to maintain stability (Ye and Zhao 2023). What Weibo and Yumi's company did was exactly that: to quell potential instability—the public anger. As a result, both platforms and state authorities usually resort to banning accused accounts swiftly and spare the effort to seek truth—which will mean letting public opinion fester—when dealing with accusatory reports. These fast institutional reactions encourage fans to use accusatory reporting to fabricate accusations against their enemies, making the hindrance of their real life a more severe punishment than the account blocking on the internet.

Thus, the growing victim numbers of collective reporting, as with Yumi's case, is partly a result of the internalization of the accusatory reporting strategy as a code of conduct for fans dealing with conflicts. An uncertain and vague censorship mechanism has given rise to different imaginations of censoring among social media users, and the authorities are unwilling and fail to take effective measures to manage accusatory collective reporting. They even allow users to fight each other's opponents to strengthen state control of the Chinese internet (Luo and Li 2022). This case vividly shows us a grim landscape of the social media ecology in China, where the lives of fan victims are overlooked. We feel obligated to call attention to these tragic experiences of individual fans in the conceptualization of participatory censorship and fandom nationalism in our primer and ethnographic research.

Nationalistic Participatory Censorship

In the previous two sections, we introduced the representative fan practice of accusatory reporting in Chinese fandom and explained the concept of participatory censorship. But how can we understand this practice as participatory censorship in Zhang's cancellation caused by nationalism? How does this understanding bring complexities and nuances to the prior conceptualization of fandom nationalism demonstrated in "The Rising Entanglement of Fandom and Nationalism" from this book's Introduction (see Figure 0.1)?

The prior conceptualization of fandom nationalism demonstrated in the model in Figure 0.1 can help explain most of the incident's development in the later stage of Zhang's cancellation, when common Chinese social media users joined the movement to boycott Zhang for his perceived betrayal of the nation. As the incident developed, the state—represented by state-run media—made explicit such sentiments and practices, which strengthened the mainstream patriotic narrative. As shown in Chapter 2, soon after the "worship devil" accusation surfaced and prevailed, common Chinese social media users joined the anti-fans to collectively condemn Zhang, and the state media set the tone of this incident with their strongly worded commentaries. After August 13, 2021, Zhang's own Weibo account was blocked, and more platforms removed his works. Such negative public opinion prevailed and was very hard to reverse, especially as Zhang was censored and had no channel to explain himself. This censorship even extended to the online shopping realm, which had become a standard industry practice when celebrities or brands got into trouble (Huang and Janssen 2019; Ng 2022). Taobao and Goofish blocked the keyword "Zhang Zhehan" from their search results. Thus, when fans searched for products related to Zhang, they were shown "can't find any product."

Not only was Zhang a target of nationalist participatory censorship, Zhang's fans, too, fell victim to such practices. Nationalist participants posted harsh comments on their Weibo accounts, formed online "eradicating-traitor squads," and reported Zhang's supporters' accounts to authorities for further censorship. On the day the photos of the Yasukuni Shrine were exposed, Zhang's big fans called on the not-yet-eliminated fans' super topic platform to refrain from speaking and quietly wait for Zhang's response. BL-adapted stars like Zhang tend to have many young girls among their fans who are not sensitive to political topics and social public events and are prone to make "wrong" comments in their rush to defend their idols, thus intensifying the social media users' hatred for Zhang. On the night of August 12, Zhang's big fans spoke out urgently on Weibo:

> Don't speak, stay silent, this is not something fans can clarify. Be aware of the seriousness of the incident, don't make the mistake of passing the blade to anti-fans. Lie flat and take the beating, the only thing fans can do for him is to stop adding to the trouble.

The big fans, who had been at the vanguard of previous clashes with anti-fans, and who continued voicing their support for Zhang, more easily fell targets of trolling, harassment, accusatory reporting, and even threats of physical harm. Our informant Rose, who was one of Zhang's big fans (only-fans) and had been persistently vocal during this incident, urged ordinary fans to remain sensible and silent, and to make sure not to make childish comments on key patriotic issues that could bring bad publicity to Zhang. From August to December 2021, Rose's four Weibo accounts were reported and blocked. After each account was blocked by the platform, Rose would register a new account again using different identity information and continue to speak. She explained, "I've been 'reincarnated' four times, account banning is routine for me now" (Rose, in-person interview, Shanghai, October 18, 2021). In both Zhang's and his fans' experiences, we can see how the fan and fan-like practices of participatory censorship can be incorporated and exploited by the state to strengthen its nationalist narrative. However, we should not ignore how participatory censorship also can manifest in other ways in our case study.

Zhang's cancellation took place because of an environment that is primed by the routinization of accusatory reporting that we described earlier in "Rivalries and Fan Wars". We can see that, by creating guidebooks and strategically using nationalistic accusations—such as history nihilism—to win fan wars, fans are more than mere passive actors who are shaped and exploited by the state's nationalistic narrative. Rather, they show agency in conducting participatory censorship with accusatory reporting. In our case study, on August 12, before Zhang's photo outside Yasukuni Shrine was exposed, anonymous posts appeared on both Douban and Weibo, revealing photos where Zhang was photographed with Madam Dewi, one of the wedding guests, when attending a friend's wedding in Japan in 2019. The post highlighted that Dewi is the wife of President Sukarno, who massacred the Chinese in Indonesia, and accused Zhang of having a pro-Japanese and anti-Chinese stance (see Figure 3.3). Although there was clarification later that the president who led the anti-Chinese massacre in Indonesia was not Dewi's husband, previous distorted and exaggerated posts became "evidence" of Zhang being a national traitor and were widely disseminated throughout the course of development in Zhang's cancellation, which generated collective outrage.

[A Marketing Account]
8-13 11:49

Yesterday, I saw a netizen exposing that he previously attended a friend's wedding in Japan. Both the couple are Chinese (the groom has 1/4 Japanese ancestry), and the bride is from Dalian. They held a traditional Japanese wedding at the Nogi Shrine in Japan (which honors the World War II war criminal Noguchi Maresuke). During the wedding, Zhang Zhehan took a photo with the former First Lady of Indonesia, Madam Dewi (her husband, former Indonesian President Sukarno, was responsible for the massacre of Chinese people). ...
#ZhangZhehanYasukuniShrine

FIGURE 3.3A AND 3.3B *The marketing account published a photo of Zhang with Mrs. Dewi and accused Zhang of having a pro-Japanese stance. Captured by the first author on August 16, 2021.*

In recent years, mainstream nationalist narratives have given rise to the popular conspiratory framework among a radical contingent of Chinese citizens that some people of influence are bought by foreign enemies to work as spies inside and against China, which has been conveniently adopted by the fandom communities. If there was any continuation of state-sponsored violence during the reform period of China (Dutton 2008), it manifested as a shift that did not focus on the traditional distinction between friend and enemy but rather on the social divide between legality and illegality. The power of this mimetic revolution could dissipate or channel any signs of intensity into legal frameworks. Such fandom nationalistic actions are like "mimetic revolutions." The anti-fans' predominant strategy was to dichotomize "us" (righteous patriots) and "them" (national traitors) as antagonistic to each other. Therefore, in the accusatory reports and argumentation for the cancellation of certain celebrities, such conspiratory narratives are often strategically used. This is also the case in our case study and fandom nationalism cases in general. By adopting such narratives, the anti-fans strategically establish a dichotomy between *us* and *them*—in this case, the righteous patriots and the evil national traitors, which allows the anti-fans to level up conflicts in/between fan communities to being conflicts about national interests. Usually, accusations of celebrities being traitors and spies are easily accepted and embraced by Chinese citizens, as such "us versus them" nationalist narratives have been prevailing in Chinese society (Huang 2023; Zhang and Shroeder 2024). Through this rhetoric, nationalist citizens themselves become more susceptible to manipulation and mobilization. This technique effectively exploits divisions within the fan community and channels them into a narrative of justice versus injustice, ultimately influencing the perception of nationalist citizens. In this way, fan communities take advantage of nationalistic narratives, nationalist Chinese citizens, and the Party-State, in order to win their own battles. Therefore, we should update the fandom nationalism model by separating citizens and fan communities into different stakeholders, and by adding fan communities' strategization and exploitation of nationalistic narratives into the dynamics.

Once we treat nationalist citizens and fan communities as two separate stakeholders, we should also reconsider the state's role and its relationship with others in this model. In our conceptualization of participatory censorship, we emphasize one crucial element in definition: the alignment with the interests, narrative, values, and norms of power holders. Compared to direct state censorship, participatory censorship does not revolve around the state. Rather, the state has power over other stakeholders by dominating the narratives, norms, and ideologies, as well as limiting other stakeholders in its legal and political frameworks. In Zhang's incident, and similar fandom nationalism cases in China, the ultimate power holder is the Party-State. Therefore, the updated model of fandom nationalism should demonstrate the Party-State as a structural stakeholder. One such structure is nationalism ideology, as discussed extensively in previous chapters, and the other is the distrust in—to a certain extent even hostility against—fandom culture.

Misconceptions and misrepresentations of fandom culture—especially idol fandoms—are widespread in Chinese mainstream media and society. Public opinion is largely bent on ridiculing and criticizing fandom culture, which leads to the unsubstantiated discreditation of fans' perspectives, opinions, and argumentation (Wang and Ge 2023). This is well illustrated in the previously mentioned CAC's "sweep-up campaigns" since June 2021, where online fan communities are targeted for their perceived harmful behaviors (CAC 2021a). In relevant social media heated discussions, the expression of "fandom mindset" has become trendy and has frequently been employed derogatorily by non-fan Chinese citizens and state media to condemn fans for their "crazy" and "irrational" actions (Ge and Wang 2023). This predisposition to distrust fans in Chinese mainstream society makes it hard for the idol fans to defend their idols and themselves when controversies and misinformation happen. For the general public, idols poison the nation's youths, the fandom culture is toxic, and therefore fans and fandom culture deserve criticism, ridicule, and punishment, just as the state insisted. Specifically, female fans of male pop idols are further stigmatized and marginalized as *fanquannvhai* (fandom girls) who are crazy consumers brainwashed by the idol industry and who thus cannot discern right from wrong (e.g., Tencent 2021).[4] Therefore, the Chinese mainstream patriarchal perspective on female-dominated fandom culture is extremely negative, rendering insufficient respect, trust, and tolerance for fans' opinions and argumentation. In this case, mainstream Chinese society is ready to eliminate the so-deemed "toxic" idol culture and show no mercy to Zhang or his fans when accusations against his perceived problematic political stance surface.

Fans' Resistance to Participatory Censorship in Zhang's Incident

Due to such mistrust and marginalization, there is an added layer of censorship, as these fans are under more risk if they speak up to defend their idol, which might serve to silence these fans. Outspoken fans face trolling, harassment, and even threats to their safety. The fan identity makes fans' defense and explanation untrustworthy. The internet slang of *jianfenji* (identifying fan domicile) refers to non-fan social media users' practice of trying to identify whether a user who speaks up is part of someone's fandom before being granted credibility. Once the user is found to be a fan, what they say will be generalized as a fan blindly defending an idol

---

[4] https://new.qq.com/rain/a/20210926A08R7P00 (Retrieved August 20, 2024).

and will not be taken seriously. Therefore, when the media reports scandalous news about an idol, fans usually hesitate to defend the idol en masse, as this is likely to have a negative effect and lead to the idol being perceived in an even worse way by the mainstream society.

"I feel like I've become an enemy of the nation," informant Wendy said in tears after Zhang's case. Wendy is one of the five members in the Zhang only-fans WeChat group. She was also a university student living with her parents and inevitably discussed the events of Zhang, the biggest news in the entertainment industry at the time, at school and at home, revealing that she tended to clash with her classmates and family.

> I'm starting to wonder if my judgement is wrong. Why is it that the whole society, the whole Internet, and even my family hold views contrary to mine, and I really can't hold on to them anymore!
>
> (Wendy, in-person interview, September 27, 2021, Changsha, China)

Wendy's heartfelt comments represent the state of mind of a large group of Zhang's fans at the time, who did not believe Zhang's allegations and who always believed that he was wrongly accused, and who even encountered cyberbullying from nationalist citizens on Weibo when defending Zhang. It was particularly devastating to see their idol's future ruined by a smear campaign at the height of his popularity.

Throughout the process of Zhang's banning, our five-member WeChat group was immersed in an atmosphere of sadness, with the feeling that Zhang had been wronged, but unable to defend him on public platforms due to their own fan status—the status of fan seemed to lead to an instant judgment by the public. Informants Tina and Silvia even showed symptoms of depression at one point and needed to seek help from a psychiatrist. As they said in the WeChat group discussion:

I'm disappointed to the core with the entertainment industry in this country. I'm willing to continue to be a fan of the domestic entertainment industry if he comes back one day. But if he just disappears, I'll just go and love foreign stars.
(Tina, WeChat group conversation, August 23, 2021)

Ugh, I often feel like I've come out of it, but I always feel sad when I see those big celebrity parties where there should have been one seat for him too.
(Silvia, WeChat group conversation, September 3, 2021)

As the targets of collective action triggered by nationalism that aligns with the Party-State's ideology, Zhang's fans have turned to a more secretive and private community that is rarely seen by the general public, creating new spaces for communication among mutually trusted fans. They formed smaller, more closed groups within the fan community, such as the five-member WeChat group that our informants created.

Just as with any form of censorship, fandom nationalism as a form of participatory censorship is not met without resistance. Facing the aftermath of Zhang's accident, Zhang's fans self-organized, reflected on various political ideologies and concepts, and reaffirmed their fan identities.

While fragmented into smaller groups, big fans in the original fan community continued their responsibilities and guided the common fans to navigate the situation, as a large number of common fans could not afford to seek out a more private and secluded sub-community. Faced with the imminent threat of their idol being banned, fans can quickly reach a consensus and employ top-down strategies to combat platform erasure in the shortest possible time. Experienced big fans, through daily experimentation with the censorship system within fandom, have compiled effective "(counter-) reporting guidebooks." As a result, accurate predictions regarding the steps leading to a ban can be made, enabling their proactive responses. As informant Rose aptly stated,

"When we understand what content will be reported, we also know how to avoid it" (Rose, in-person interview, Shanghai, June 29, 2021). Thus, in contrast to the participatory censorship examined in the previous section, when fans have to stand against the state, these "reporting guidebooks" serve the opposite purpose—guiding fans on how to evade censorship. This showcases the counter-public traits (Fraser 1990; Downey and Fenton 2003; Dahlberg 2007) of fan culture in China (e.g., Hu and Wang 2021; Liao et al. 2022), just as other fan studies scholars identified in Western fandoms (e.g., Jenkins 1992; Stanfill 2019). The multiple public spheres, including a dominant one and several "subaltern counter-publics" (Fraser 1990, 80), are alternative discursive arenas where marginalized groups develop oppositional interpretations of their identities, interests, and needs, which expand discursive space to address their exclusion from the dominant public sphere. The counter-public sphere often challenges hegemonic discourse by incorporating dissenting voices (Warner 2021). Higher-ranking fans, such as the administrators of fan clubs, have direct contact with idol talent agencies, enabling top-down guidance from the company's perspective to encourage fan participation in collective action, while also providing a channel for bottom-up feedback from common fans.

When commenting on Zhang's cancellation, fans not only use abbreviations or homophonic replacements to evade censorship triggered by sensitive keywords but they also reflect on political issues. To protect their identities, we only present the paraphrased quotes from fans' posts and comments instead of using screenshots from Weibo.

It's terrifying; it's like a replay of the WG [an abbreviation for the Cultural Revolution in Chinese, *wen ge*].

Is it necessary to censor to this extent? They treat him as if he were a real traitor to the nation. This is no longer normal cultural governance. It is a witch hunt orgy.

His name has become a banned sensitive word. What should people with the same name as him do?

Just based on a photo of journey, they can pass a "death sentence" on a public figure without any investigation. Is this really a 皿煮FZ society? [皿煮 is the homophonic word for "democracy" in Chinese; FZ is an abbreviation for "rule of law"].

As our informant Tina told us during an in-person meeting after the Zhang incident:

I have always been a well-behaved "good kid." I live here and can watch dramas, follow idols, and attend my brother's concerts. I was content. But since he got into trouble, I experienced for the first time that the entertainment industry was a cutthroat place. It's good that he left now. It would be even better if he could go abroad, to a freer country, to study the theatre arts he loves and live a freer life, never to return.

(Tina, in-person interview, Changsha, October 17, 2021)

Within their own cultural context, fans use familiar discourses to interpret grand political concepts. They use their own language to dilute the grand narratives, placing concepts such as "nationalism," "patriotism," "democracy," and "nation-state" within the context of fan culture and the relatively private domain of fan communities. They communicate criticism and dissatisfaction with power through various abbreviations, homophonic words, slang words, and coded language. By engaging in alternative fan strategies, fans re-evaluate the meanings of "democracy" and "nation," imbuing their fan practices with counter-public significance (Noonan 2008; Warner 2021).

Fans also found various alternative ways to consume Zhang-related content or products to reaffirm their fan identities. From August to December 2021, the only-fans of Zhang had been doing two main tasks: the first was to collect everything they could about Zhang and his films and dramas before they were erased from the internet. By the time

Zhang's apology letter was released on August 13, seeing that social media users were still in a state of angry cursing, my fan friends sadly predicted that Zhang might be boycotted and asked us to be prepared to download as soon as possible any films, dramas, variety shows, interviews, magazine photos, and fan-made videos featuring him. Rose told us that it seemed that by downloading and collecting in this way, she was able to alleviate some of the hurt she had suffered in this boycott, and that those happy memories of her own past were still available to be revisited in secret, "As long as I keep remembering him, discussing him, and loving him, he hasn't disappeared from this cyber world" (Rose, in-person interview, Shanghai, October 18, 2021).

These preparations were also called for by big fans and widely accepted among Zhang's fan community, with fans even flocking to the online shopping platform Taobao to buy mobile hard drives in bulk to store available data related to Zhang. At that time, the Taobao shop of Seagate (a brand of mobile hard drives) sold out of its entire stock. On the night of August 14, we observed that Seagate's live-streaming page on Taobao was suddenly flooded with over 20,000 viewers; the live-streamer confirmed that it was ten times the number of previous viewers. Faced with such traffic, Seagate's live-streamer asked: "Where did you all come from? Why are so many people coming to buy mobile hard drives tonight?" Zhang's fans, in turn, replied in the room:

> Don't ask questions, just focus on selling stuff.
> You're blessed to be here, don't ask anything else.
> We can't talk about it for fear that your live stream room will be banned.
>
> (Public conversation in live-stream, Taobao.com, August 14, 2021)

The fans who collectively bought the mobile hard drives formed a tacit agreement, choosing to silently buy up

Seagate's stock in order not to reveal keywords and have their live-streams banned if detected by the platform algorithm, leaving only a confused but fortunate live-streamer.

Meanwhile, fans quickly searched the second-hand market for Zhang's related merchandise. Our informants, Rose, Silvia, and Tina, diligently searched for various keywords related to Zhang on goofish.com (the second-hand trading platform) from August 15 to early September. Every day, they aimed to collect as many second-hand magazines, endorsed products, photo-books, and related items as possible because these items were no longer available through official channels, and fans anticipated that Zhang might never be seen in public again. Starting on August 14, 2021, our informant set up a sharing group on Baidu Drive, storing over 200GB of Zhang's content. This is one of the examples of collective efforts by Zhang's fans, who set up a public sharing group and uploaded a portion of their own collection. On the same day, almost all of Zhang's films and TV series, interviews, photoshoots, songs, and commercials from his ten years as an actor were collected in full by Zhang's fans and circulated within the fandom. However, this kind of sharing within the community could not escape the monitoring of the online platform, and from August 20, Baidu.com began to delete users' uploads with the keyword "Zhang Zhehan." Zhang's fans then invented a countermeasure by changing the name of the profile to Zhang's alias—after this method also gradually stopped working, fans found the next place to store and share resources, Xunlei.com, and started uploading and downloading Zhang's documents on Xunlei.com.

Zhang's fans on Weibo, despite choosing to remain silent about the incident itself, continue to seek solace by sharing Zhang's photos and videos in their communities. To escape censorship from the platform and nationalist citizens, such shares are often chopped up images showing only Zhang's hands or lips, making them unrecognizable to outsiders (see Figure 3.4). The fans then resorted to new tactics to escape such blocking by replacing Zhang's name with nicknames that only fans were familiar with, such as the fans' love names of "Gardenia," "Teacher Zhang," or "wife." To date, using these coded words, it is still possible to find Zhang-related items being traded.

These fans self-deprecatingly refer to themselves as "homeless nomads" in the digital world, migrating between different online platforms, searching for traces of their idol,

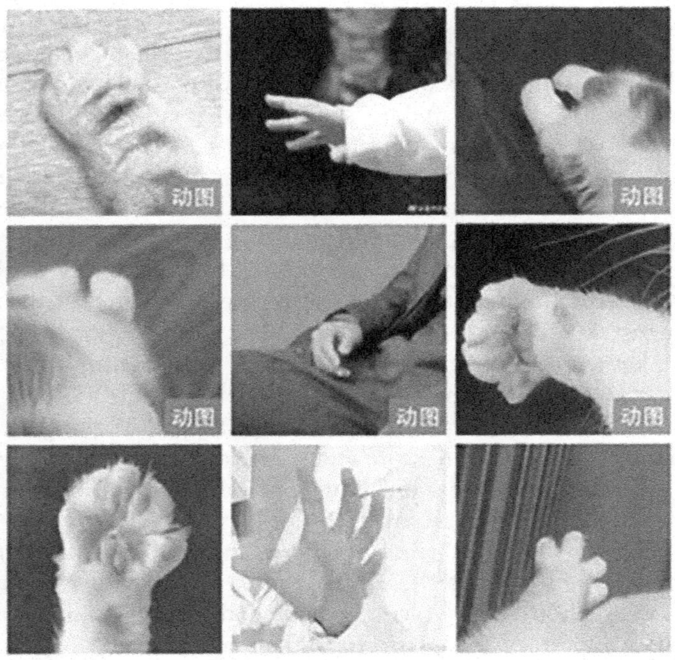

FIGURE 3.4 *Post circulated in the fan community with three photos of Zhang's hands alongside six photos of cats' paws. Captured by the first author on August 23, 2021.*

and collecting this fragmented data like prey, bringing it back to share within their own communities. In this fan practice, Zhang seems to have become a fragmented, symbolized idol, a "you-know-who" that exists in Chinese fan culture. By being such homeless nomads, Zhang's fans reaffirm their fan identities.

What we have presented in this section and chapter is our first update to the theorization of fandom nationalism by introducing, developing, and contextualizing the concept of participatory censorship to understand this phenomenon. Here, we illustrate this update in Figure 3.5. In fandom nationalism, participants perform participatory censorship, which is the practice of (anti-)fans and nationalist citizens voluntarily engaging in participatory practices—such as accusatory reporting—with the intention to destroy an idol and their fandom, or to reinforce patriotism in society by aligning with the Party-State's nationalist ideology. The Party-State imposes

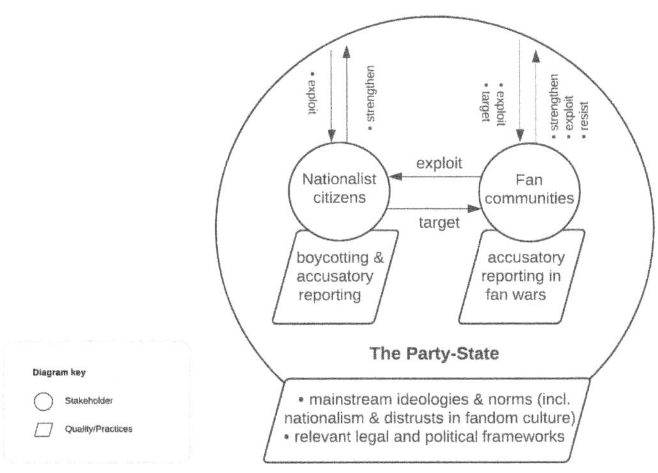

FIGURE 3.5 *Updated model of fandom nationalism. Made by the authors.*

its power by structuring how such practices are enabled or limited by mainstream ideologies as well as political and legal institutions. However, even restricted by such structures, fans still manage to participate in resistance and reaffirm their fan identities.

CHAPTER FOUR

Performative Patriotism

Multi-stakeholders' Engagement with Fandom Nationalism

In the last chapter, we focused on the practices of participatory censorship and the dynamics between the more obvious stakeholders in fandom nationalism: fans, nationalist citizens, and the state. However, there is an important type of stakeholder missing in this model: the commercial entities and businesses. In Zhang's case and fandom nationalism cases alike, two representative stakeholders of such are social media platforms and brands.

Social media platforms as a stakeholder—Weibo in Zhang's incident and many other cancellation cases—play a role in shaping fandom nationalism, meaning that they afford and limit how users interact on these platforms. Social media platforms are profit-driven private companies that are dominated by the social media logic of popularity and datafication, where the standardized metrics to evaluate accounts and their content rule the economic transactions and thus users' behaviors and interactions (van Dijck and Poell 2013). This logic compels social media platforms to embrace and accommodate fan economy and fandom practices, as fans' interactions with each other and their fan subjects—in this case the idol—generate immense traffic and thus advertisement revenues for the platforms (Zhang and Negus 2020; Yin and Xie 2024). Meanwhile, Chinese platforms are embedded in the Chinese sociopolitical context and constrained by the Party-State's power and regulations, which means that they also carefully conduct self-governance to avoid the state's wrath while maximizing their user engagement and profit (Ye et al. 2024). For instance, as introduced in "Canceled: The Consequences of Nationalist Fan Mobilization", just one day after Zhang issued his apology, Weibo banned both Zhang's and his studio's accounts. Even the novelist Zhan An, who defended Zhang on Weibo, was banned immediately (see Table 2.1 in Chapter 2). Simultaneously, the hashtag #*CCDI comment on Zhang's incident* reached the top of Weibo's trending topics. These reactions are believed to demonstrate Weibo's rapid and careful self-governance in sensitive situations to avoid larger-scale negative repercussions.

Brands are playing crucial roles in fandom nationalism too. Fandom researchers have been paying attention to how the media industries and businesses manipulate and exploit fans for economic gains (Stanfill 2019; Cui and Wu 2024). Specifically, the trend of queer baiting has been on the rise globally (Brennan 2018; Abidin 2019), including China (Zheng 2024). This is especially evident in how brands engage with BL-adapted-drama fandoms, such as Zhang's fans and *The Word of Honor*'s fans. Before the scandal erupted, sponsors and endorsers were actively investing in the two male stars, with their popularity yielding substantial economic benefits. For example, the fashion magazine *Harper's Bazaar* produced an electronic magazine featuring these two male stars as a couple, which, as of March 18, 2021, had nearly 231,000 sales, generating over 1.38 million RMB (around $193,553).[1] Since the premiere of *The Word of Honor* on

---

[1]https://www.mad-men.com/articldetails/12455 (Retrieved September 3, 2024).

February 21, 2021, Zhang and Gong had announced eight new endorsements by March 26 (Sohu.com, 2021).[2] However, what will brands do when the idols and their fandoms get involved in controversies, especially the ones that do not align with the state's ideologies or mainstream norms, such as patriotism? How do fans respond to brands' actions? How should we understand these dynamics? In this chapter, we shift our attention to these aspects in fandom nationalism.

Conceptualize Performative Patriotism

As we discussed before, patriotism is a state-endorsed mainstream ideology in China. However, there have always been tensions between the state and the grassroots regarding how patriotism should look and be practiced (Zhang and Ma 2023). In 2021, the Communist Youth League of China even published a commentary to criticize "patriotism business," the phenomenon of some content creators attempting to use patriotism as their selling point to obtain more views and likes (Communist Youth League of China 2021). The framing of "patriotism business" highlights several characteristics of such patriotic practices: profit-driven, insincere, and embedded in the social media business logic.

These characteristics coincide with findings in previous research about social movements on social media platforms. Scholars coin the term "performative allyship" or "performative activism" to express concerns and criticism about the shallow and artificial online participations in social movements with the primary intention to obtain social and economic capital (Qin 2022; Thimsen 2022; Wellman 2022; Spielmann et al. 2023). These concerns and criticisms are echoed in various research about social movements and digital technologies,

---

[2]https://www.sohu.com/a/457413922_121075791 (Retrieved September 3, 2024).

among which Banet-Weiser's (2018) discussion on politics and economy of visibility provides a good framework to understand the structural issues in this phenomenon. Visibility is a means to an end in political movements as it can bring attention to the matter and potentially lead to productive social change (2018). However, visibility has become an end in itself in these political movements as it can also generate business profits and accumulate social capital (2018). Therefore, the term "performative" perfectly captures individuals' or entities' participation in digital movements in pursuit of visibility as an end.

However, the term "performative" bears multi-layered meanings in different contexts. In research about performative allyship or activism, the term is used in a way closer to its pejorative meaning in popular conception, emphasizing and criticizing the gap between someone's speech, actions, and intentions (Blair 2021). However, in conventional academic discussion, the word often focuses on the gap between utterances and their effects (Blair 2021) or can be traced back to Goffman's (2023) theatrical metaphor of performance, referring to the presentations and actions through which individuals construct various identities to achieve success in different social interactions and environments. Researchers have also followed such a conceptualization and have discussed patriotism/nationalism as performative. Johnston (2024) follows Billig's (2005) analysis of banal nationalism and presents the performative patriotism in MAGA movements as "a repertoire of behaviors mostly benign, easy to embrace, and act out," to guide "ritualistic affirmations of their national identity" (410–11). Similarly, Nosal and colleagues (2021) as well as Cole (2024) discuss football fans' practices and how they can be understood as a performative nationalism, which includes their expression of local and national identities through performative display and tools, such as banners, chants, choreographies, and marches.

Tapping into the multi-layered meaning of the term "performative," and informed by previous work on Chinese fandom nationalism (Gong 2022), we conceptualize the practices of and dynamics between different stakeholders in Zhang's cancellation incident and cases alike as performative patriotism. This refers to individuals' or organizations' performative display and ritualistic affirmation of their national identity and pride, with the intention of transforming garnered visibility on social media platforms to economic or social capital (either for themselves or for someone else), while also ensuring that their stance remains aligned with the Chinese state to avoid potential complications. In the context of our study of fandom nationalism, such performative patriotism is structured by the social media platforms' business logic. Adding to this aspect, our second update to the model of fandom nationalism further complicates the dynamics with multi-stakeholders' positions and practices, which is illustrated in Figure 0.3 and explained in detail through our ethnographic data in Zhang's incident.

Businesses Perform Patriotism for Capital

Let's first take a look at how the added crucial stakeholder in this model—businesses—perform patriotism for their profit in Zhang's cancellation. As described in previous chapters, soon after the accusation about Zhang surfaced and prevailed, Zhang was condemned and banned by state institutions and the entertainment industry. Amid these tensions, there were a large number of companies immediately announcing they would cut ties and stop endorsement and any form of collaboration with Zhang, as national interest is above everything, and that they do not tolerate immoral and unpatriotic celebrities. These companies won the praise of nationalist citizens and were even able to attract them to spend money in support of these "patriotic businessmen." Marketing media accounts were also actively involved in fabricating and spreading more rumors and disinformation about Zhang to entice nationalist citizens to boost the accounts' engagement, which could then turn into social or economic capital. Thus, rumors and disinformation about Zhang did not stop with his disappearance from social media platforms and the entertainment industry; rather, they evolved and spread with greater exaggeration. Since August 13, 2021, when Zhang's photos were exposed, together with our fan informants, we witnessed how businesses co-constructed the censorship and prosecution of Zhang in the name of patriotism.

On the night of August 12, only-fans who stayed up all night following the social media users' accusations were also worried about something else: the fear that Zhang's sponsors would terminate collaboration contracts with him en masse. This had happened before with banned celebrities. When a celebrity is popular, sponsors flock to invite them into short-term commercial endorsements and advertisements. As soon as a scandal emerges about the celebrity, the sponsors usually immediately announce the termination of such contracts on Weibo to distance themselves from the star's behavior. The brands that quickly announce their termination are often enthusiastically supported by nationalist citizens through consumption, who are even attracted to spend money on their products—a lucrative performance and a cruel trigger for yet another wave of cyberbullying against the celebrity and their fans.

Unsurprisingly, on the morning of August 13, after Zhang posted his apology on Weibo, the nationalist citizens' anger was still not quelled and the appeals for Zhang to be banned grew even louder. Having observed such public responses, the brands that had previously sponsored or collaborated with Zhang raced to announce the termination of their contracts and business relationships. Beverage brand Wahaha was the first to announce the termination of its contract with Zhang—he issued his apology at 6:00 a.m., and Wahaha's Weibo account announced the termination at 10:30 a.m. The comments under this Weibo post with the highest number of likes and replies were all praises for the brand for being the first to act and calls to buy more Wahaha products (see Figure 4.1).

Following Wahaha, other brands also announced the termination of their contracts with Zhang in the shortest possible time. These waves of termination acted as a conviction of Zhang commercially, pushing him and his fans into confrontation with mainstream opinion. In our small group of five Zhang only-fans, we recorded this discussion (August 13, 2021, WeChat group). Rose said angrily: "A bunch of cold-blooded, heartless vampires! Especially the brand XXX, whose Weibo account was affectionately calling fans 'sisters' before Zhang's accident, and now they've immediately abandoned us!" "Sponsors cannot be trusted, they treat their fans like 'leeks,'"[3] Tina replied. "These sponsors are really evil, the fans are just the dumbest people and call them 'moneymaker daddies,' where is the dad to abandon his kids firstly in a disaster?" Tina continued. Yumi replied,

It's really a very tricky and toxic strategy. These sponsors run the fan economy when the stars are popular, milking the fans dry to attract them to buy the products in bulk. But when the star is in a disaster, they immediately jump in to draw a line and perform their patriotism, so they attract another group of non-fans to buy their products in large quantities!

---

[3] "Cutting leeks" (割韭菜) is a common term in Chinese internet slang to describe marketing practices that focus on short-term profits without a long-term development plan. Because leeks are a very hardy vegetable, when the leaves are cut off from the root and sold, they will soon grow back. Just like a steady stream of fans from one generation to the next, sponsors invite the popular stars to endorse their products, thinking only about how they can drain the fans' pockets of every penny in the short term, without any thought of developing long-term loyal customers. The financial situation and sustainability of the fans are not respected.

Tina added,

A wave of cutting fans' leeks when they sign up the contracts, and a wave of cutting social media users' leeks when they terminate their contracts, win-win! Really cold-blooded and ruthless vampires!

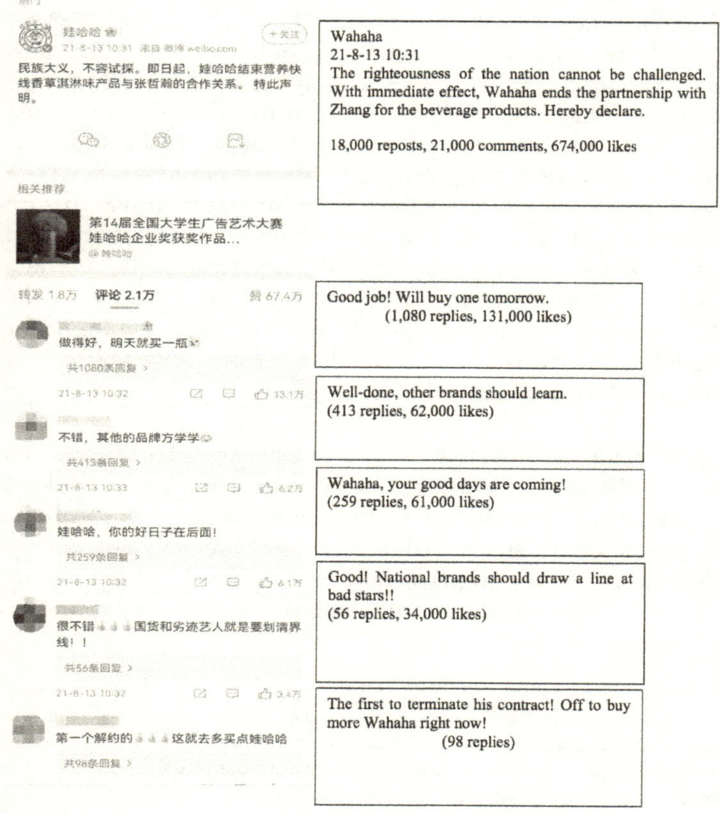

Wahaha
21-8-13 10:31
The righteousness of the nation cannot be challenged. With immediate effect, Wahaha ends the partnership with Zhang for the beverage products. Hereby declare.

18,000 reposts, 21,000 comments, 674,000 likes

Good job! Will buy one tomorrow.
(1,080 replies, 131,000 likes)

Well-done, other brands should learn.
(413 replies, 62,000 likes)

Wahaha, your good days are coming!
(259 replies, 61,000 likes)

Good! National brands should draw a line at bad stars!!
(56 replies, 34,000 likes)

The first to terminate his contract! Off to buy more Wahaha right now!
(98 replies)

FIGURE 4.1 *Wahaha announcing that it had terminated its contract with Zhang on August 13, 2021. Captured by the first author on December 21, 2022.*

Abby commented self-deprecatingly,

Isn't it a bit unhelpful that we only saw the true face of the capitalists when we reached the moment that our "house collapsed" [refers to idol having scandals]? From now on, no matter which star I love, I won't spend money on things for him, all this money goes into the pockets of the capitalists, and as a result, when it comes to the moment of crisis, the first ones to abandon us are also the capitalists!

The involvement of those businesses is not only reflected in the ruthless termination of sponsorship but also in the collusion between businesses and social media, where marketing accounts on social media platforms spare no effort to exaggerate and distort the facts to smear Zhang for engagement and visibility of their accounts. The marketing accounts' nationalist narratives were sometimes unvalidated rumors. One of the most widespread rumors was a photo that Zhang posted in 2019, which anti-fans used as evidence of Zhang making Nazi gestures (see Figure 4.2). Based on this claim, nationalist narratives evolved into a conspiracy theory that Zhang had always been a Japanese spy, which was believed to be true by Chinese nationalist citizens. However, according to Zhang's fans, this photo was intended to imitate an iconic pose of a character he played in a film. These unfounded allegations further reinforced Zhang's "national traitor" image among nationalist citizens, who became increasingly convinced that Zhang was guilty and deserved the punishment.

As discussed in the previous section, these businesses—including brands and marketing accounts—are afforded and structured by the business logic of the social media platform Weibo. To drive more engagement, they perform patriotism by aligning with the nationalist social media users and boosting controversies to gain more visibility, as the platform's algorithms favor accounts and content with high engagement. Marketing accounts' practices of fabricating and disseminating rumors about Zhang exacerbate participatory censorship

FIGURE 4.2 *One Weibo marketing account collating evidence about Hitler's Nazi salute and Zhang's photos. Captured by the first author on September 26, 2021.*

orchestrated in the name of patriotism. They capitalize on sensationalism and nationalist sentiments to generate traffic and engagement, thereby perpetuating the spread of unsubstantiated allegations and contributing to the escalation of online hostility.

When brands are confronted with political controversies involving celebrities in collaboration, they perform patriotism by loudly announcing the termination of the collaboration to appeal to nationalist citizens and even potentially attain the Party-State's favor. This even sparks a competition of contract terminations, where the brands that announce the termination first receive praise from nationalist citizens, while those that lag behind are questioned about their political stance. The brands' termination of sponsorship and collaboration contracts with Zhang such as Wahaha exemplifies how businesses strategically leverage nationalist discourses to bolster their own public image and market standing. By publicly disassociating themselves from Zhang's alleged misconduct, these companies sought to align themselves with prevailing nationalist sentiments, thereby garnering praise and support from nationalist citizens. This performative act of contract termination not only serves as a symbolic gesture of patriotism but also functions as a strategic maneuver to safeguard their brand reputation amidst a charged online environment. The race to be the first to sever ties with Zhang intensifies the performative nature of fandom nationalism practices and perpetuates the cycle of online violence driven by nationalist fervor.

As both the businesses and the platform benefit from sensational content—controversies and rumors about Zhang being a national traitor in this case—this content is not moderated by Weibo in a timely manner. In this way, the businesses become active actors in nurturing and amplifying fandom nationalism, being complicit in spreading rumors and disinformation. In turn, such practices of performative patriotism reinforce the Party-State's nationalist ideologies. The interplay between businesses, media, and the state power in orchestrating performative patriotism underscores the complex stakeholder involvement and dynamics at play in fandom nationalism. Performative patriotism becomes a tool through which platforms and businesses align themselves with dominant nationalist discourses and narratives, reinforcing the Party-State's ideology and influencing public opinions. Facing such a powerful alliance and collusion of the state institutions, business entities, and the mainstream society, fans feel powerless and suffer from trauma and distress.

Fans Perform Patriotism to Survive and Thrive

As we discussed in "Fans' Resistance to Participatory Censorship in Zhang's Incident", fans harness their creativity to devise alternative strategies in their battle against censorship, employing coded language and metaphors as a means to evade algorithmic censorship. Yet, amid this remarkable display of positivity, fans also struggle with a moral dilemma. Behind their outward resilience lies a constant questioning of their actions and a reflection of their own morality, borne out of the trauma caused by their idol's cancellation.

> I love him so I can fight the world. I know I'm right, but why doesn't anyone believe me? It was my love for him that kept me going to this day, otherwise I would have fallen apart.
>
> (Casual conversation, WeChat, from August to December 2021)

Almost every informant in this small WeChat group confided in us about their struggles and questioning of their own positions on this matter, even to the extent of needing to seek counseling. This results from the clash between personal moral judgment and the grand narrative in Chinese mainstream society. In China, where collective honor is advocated, conflicts between the individual and the collective can be a cruel and stressful situation for the individual. This stress largely comes from the fans' family members. All four of our informants who are Zhang fans shared with us their experiences of conflicts with their families regarding Zhang's incident. During our fieldwork in Changsha (October 3–17, 2021), we encountered Tina's father before a scheduled interview with her. He confided in us that Tina had been frequently depressed and in tears since Zhang's incident, spending a lot of money to collect products related to Zhang. Furthermore, Tina had been reprimanded by her father for criticizing the authorities' policies at home, which was deemed a dangerous and politically incorrect statement by her father. He believed that, as someone older and more educated, we would be more rational and calmer in helping him educate Tina, hoping that she would wake up soon and no longer be influenced by "the toxic idol culture." After her father left, Tina complained to us:

> My dad called Zhang a national traitor and accused me of being brainwashed by a traitorous idol. I cannot tolerate this. He even told my teacher about it, hoping that the university would keep a closer eye on me. I feel suffocated in such a family environment. No one is willing to listen to me defend Zhang. Now, I'm basically unwilling to talk to them anymore.
>
> (Tina, in-person interview, Changsha, October 17, 2021)

This ideological onslaught from family and society made the fans who became homeless nomads suffer from great mental pressure, and the fandom's alternative strategies to fight the erasure were also difficult to support in the long run. Thus, at the end of our fieldwork in 2021, when the story settled and Zhang completely disappeared from the Chinese Internet, some of his fans gradually healed themselves and began to seek new fan objects as their mental support, leaving Zhang's fandom for other stars:

> I'm relieved to know from his Instagram that he's been fine, but there is no any activity about him in the Chinese entertainment industry, so I'll go to another house [referring to another idol's fandom] temporarily and I'll be back when Zhang has any activity.
>
>   (Bella, video interview, WeChat, November 12, 2021)

Fans chose new idols with more realistic considerations: they preferred to idolize stars who were considered relatively "safer." This "safety" comes from the idols' alignment with Party-State narratives and ideologies, especially concerning political issues. For example, some informants who were once CP-fans or only-fans of Zhang have now become fans of Korean idols.

> The Korean idol industry is more mature and manages idols more strictly. They are better at keeping things confidential and the idol's persona is created more meticulously so the house rarely falls down. This Korean group I'm into now is "safer," they are very strongly for the "One China" policy and there is no risk of them having anti-Chinese views that could cause the house to fall down.
>
>   (Bella, video interview, November 12, 2021, WeChat)

> After all, "there are no idols before the state," I cannot experience any house fallen down anymore, so I need a safer idol.
>
>   (Zoe, video interview, November 17, 2021, WeChat)

"No idols before the state" is a popular slogan on Chinese social media in news concerning foreign celebrities who are regarded as anti-China. Born within Chinese fan communities during the time of the "Ban on Korean Entertainment," the slogan first came about when relations between China and South Korea became strained in 2016 due to the deployment of South Korea's THAAD system.[4] Since 2016, with the introduction of the ban, Chinese members of Korean idol groups have been leaving their groups and returning to China for their own solo careers, with Super Junior's Han Geng being the first and EXO's "Returning Four" (including Lu Han, Kris Wu, Lay Zhang, and Tao Huang) being the most influential. These Chinese idols were considered patriotic and hence given a steady stream of work opportunities due to their strong fan base, making them some of the earliest traffic idols in China (Yin 2020). The slogan "no idols before the state" began to circulate in the media and among patriotic fans (BBC 2016).[5] It gradually became the means for the stars' agencies and sponsors to demonstrate their alignment with mainstream society to gain acceptance from the state institutions and more opportunities from the market in China.

> Seriously, I think those who treat our state as an idol are quite stupid, but I have to say, after all, the state supports this and it's the safest to go with the trend of public opinion, the Internet environment nowadays is getting harder and harder to accommodate different voices, so I'm too lazy to argue with others, I might as well join them, even though I'm disguising as a nationalist haha.
>
> (Iris, video interview, September 24, 2021, Tencent Meeting)

---

[4]THAAD stands for Terminal High Altitude Area Defense. It is an American anti-ballistic missile defense system designed to shoot down short-, medium-, and intermediate-range ballistic missiles in their terminal phase (descent or re-entry) by intercepting them with a hit-to-kill approach.

[5]https://www.bbc.com/zhongwen/simp/china/2016/08/160802_guangdian_korea (Retrieved May 12, 2024).

Reporting is really efficient! Especially when attacking the enemies' political stance. While I do think it's unethical, my enemies will do the same to us if I don't.
(Hailey, in-person interview, May 4, 2021, Suzhou)

Therefore, the slogan "no idols before the state" has become so ingrained in fans' minds over the years that, as Zoe told us about her choice between Chinese and Korean idols, "political safety" becomes a worthwhile consideration in choosing an idol to support. For fans to decide on choosing an idol, it is the persona that the idols "perform" in line with mainstream ideologies that matters, instead of the true selves or sincere beliefs the idols possess. Our ethnography suggests that, after experiencing participatory censorship collectively, fans reject idols who may harm their fandom experience due to political risks and favor those idols who are produced in a more industrial way and who are therefore more sophisticated and politically sensitive.

In contrast to the selfless madness and reckless love for idols described by many fan scholars, these Chinese idol fans present a more utilitarian and opportunistic approach to their fan objects—the idols. This approach is a defense mechanism developed by Chinese fans to protect themselves from, and to relieve themselves of, mental stress. For fans who are powerless individuals when facing the Party-State and mainstream society, this is a way to save themselves from the risks of censorship and state control.

In addition, in response to censorship imposed by the powerful alliance discussed in the previous section, fans also started to engage in performative patriotism. Following the accusations concerning Zhang's problematic political stance, fans from other fandoms began to self-organize and self-censor. Zoe informed us that her fan community on the super topic platform called on all community members to check their past Weibo posts for any sensitive or politically damaging comments and delete them promptly if there were. They even contacted the idol and his company to double-check the idol's previous posts:

> The big fans of our fan club have also communicated with the talent agency, urging them to thoroughly inspect our brother's past photos, posts, and social media accounts outside the Great Firewall, and promptly remove any sensitive content. [...] The dreadful consequences brought about by Zhang's incident have really sounded the alarm for us.
>
> (Zoe, video interview, November 17, 2021, WeChat)

Such self-censorship has been normalized, and the fans regard such participation as an effective way to earn recognition and acceptance for the idol and fandom culture from the mainstream society. Fans expect these to contribute to more positive and favorable images for themselves and their idols.

In addition to weeding out potential damaging posts, fans and celebrities also perform patriotism in a more active manner. Celebrities work with their fan communities to present themselves as "safe" idols and good citizens by actively reposting state media news or posts on important national dates or events to demonstrate their patriotic stance. Such political signaling practices (Gao and Chen 2024) have been normalized and have become a compulsory gesture for celebrities and their fans to perform their patriotism on Weibo. This is also tightly linked to Weibo's affordances and algorithms. If the celebrities' (re)posts attain the most engagement, including likes, comments, and reposts, this (re)post will appear at the top of the "most popular post" chart, which will then make the celebrities more visible to the general public on Weibo. To fight for a position on this chart, fans organize themselves and repost their idols' patriotic posts. In this way, both the celebrities and their fans perform patriotism by reposting and reinforcing the state's narratives and ideologies.

Take, for example, the Weibo posting by the *People's Daily* on the ninety-first anniversary of "The 9.18 Incident" when Japan launched its invasion of China (see Figure 4.3). Its most popular reposts are topped by posts from male idols with large fandoms, accumulating over 300,000 reposts among the top three idols. Such a high volume of engagement was only achieved by the systematic campaigns organized by fans communities to repost, comment, and like their idols' patriotic Weibo posts en masse as soon as the idols repost performed patriotism by reposting from *People's Daily*. Within the fan community of the male idol "W"[6] listed on Figure 4.3, a task notification posted by one of the administrators on the day before 9.18 reads:

> [Urgent notice]: Tomorrow is a special day; everyone must strictly adhere to the ban on entertainment topics and participate in generating (good) traffic! It is expected that the People's Daily's Weibo will be reposted by our "brother," and we need everyone's support to make it on the top of the hot repost ranking! Let's all get moving!

In the comments under this task notification, we noticed that the big fans, such as our informant Iris, rallied their support and said: "Other idols will also be reposting this time, so it will be a fierce battle to show our data power! It's time to show our strength to the enemy!"

It is evident that these fans' (re)posting of patriotic content on Weibo is performative as the intention behind such practices is to gain visibility for their idols. The actual patriotic messages and ideology in the reposted content are not the primary concern for fans. This highlights the performative nature of these patriotic demonstrations in fandom nationalism on Weibo. As Iris's quote above shows, fans spare no effort to

---

[6]The idol's name "W" has been anonymized to protect the fan identity of Iris, and the screenshot has been omitted for privacy reasons.

People's Daily
2022-Sep-17 17:00

[If you remember today, please post: #Remember 9.18#]
September 18 1931, all Chinese people remember this day.
After 91 years, today's China is not the China in 1931. We
strengthen ourselves and revitalise China!

[Picture: DO NOT FORGET 9.18
91st Anniversary of 9.18 Incident]

8,250,000+ reposts, 93,000+ comments, 550,000+ likes
(Most repost ranking)
Li Xian
Xiao Zhan
Gong Jun
Wang Yibo
Cai Xukun
…

FIGURE 4.3 *Post by* People's Daily *on the ninety-first anniversary of "The 9.18 Incident," with the most popular repost rankings of five male stars. Captured by the first author on January 14, 2023.*[7]

[7]Xiao Zhan, who was deeply affected by "The 227 Incident," appears in this list, and it took almost a year for him to reappear in the public eye. The difference between Xiao's case and Zhang's is that Xiao was never boycotted by the authorities, so his Weibo account and his fan community still existed and were active again on the internet in September 2022, as shown in the picture.

construct a patriotic persona for their idols to ensure such a persona can be accepted by nationalist citizens, mainstream society, and the Party-State.

Another example that took place in the same period was a notice on the super topic platform of the idol group INTO1 (provided by informant Zoe; see Figure 4.4). This notice was jointly issued by the big fans who were administrators of the super topic management group, asking all fans not to post entertainment-related content on September 18. This organized self-censorship aimed to "prohibit the publication and dissemination of any content of a promotion or entertainment nature in any form." At the end of the announcement, a slogan was added: "Learn from history, be mindful of peace, and strengthen our China with all our wills." Our informant Meg also explained to us:

> I know it's a bit silly for us to impose these bans on entertainment-related content. There is no explicit policy that entertainment topics cannot be discussed on the 9.18 anniversary. But it is important to show a patriotic stance to outsiders. It can increase their favorability towards the idol, and at the same time, it can also prevent anti-fans from finding a weak point to attack.
>
> (Meg, Tianjin, August 3, 2021)

One significant aspect of performative patriotism observed among fans is the use of coded language and symbolic gestures to navigate censorship and express criticism toward prevailing political narratives. Fans often employ abbreviations, homophonic replacements, and slang words to evade online scrutiny and communicate dissatisfaction with the state's cultural governance practices. This strategic use of language serves to dilute grand political concepts such as nationalism and patriotism within the more intimate domain of fan culture, reshaping these narratives to align with their own values and interpretations.

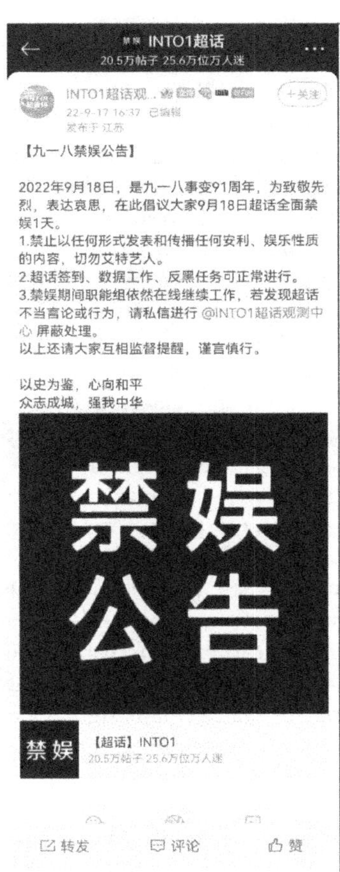

The figure's right-hand column (English translation printed alongside the image):

INTO1 super topic
205000+ posts, 256000+ members
INTO1 Super Topic Management Group
2022-Sep-17 16:37
[9.18 Prohibition of Entertainment Notice]
September 18, 2022 marks the 91st anniversary of the 9.18 Incident. To pay tribute to our martyrs and express our condolences, we hereby advocate a total ban on entertainment news on September 18 for one day on our super topic page.
1. It is forbidden to publish and disseminate any content of a promotional or entertaining nature in any form. Do not mention our idol's name.
2. Super topic sign-in, data labour and anti-black tasks can be carried out normally.
3. The management groups during the prohibition will still continue to work. If you find any inappropriate comments in the super topic, please write to us privately to block them from our super topic webpage. Please also monitor and remind each other of the above and be careful with your words.

Learn from history, be mindful of peace
Strengthen our China with all our wills.

FIGURE 4.4 *"9.18 Prohibition of Entertainment Notice" launched by the super topic management group of INTO1. Provided by informant Zoe.*

By collectively performing patriotism in this way, fans ensure the safe existence of their idols and communities, as it avoids the public's doubts and criticisms about their political stance and patriotism. These patriotic performances, in which idols and fans participate together, constitute a unique landscape of interaction between Chinese fan culture, state power, and the nationalistic sentiment of the public. The collaborative efforts between celebrities and their fan communities to project a patriotic image to the public, particularly through reposting news on significant national events or dates, exemplify the interplay between performative practices and broader cultural narratives that are structured by platform logic. The competitive repost rankings and charts on platforms like Weibo turn patriotic practices into a venue for engagement and visibility, reinforcing fans' collective identity and shaping fan practices in the digital public sphere. The proactive measures taken by fan communities, such as banning entertainment-related activities on historically significant dates, highlight the strategic alignment of fan practices with the state's ideology. Such dynamics are also corroborated by up-to-date quantitative research by Gao and Chen (2024), which demonstrates celebrities' and their fans' utilitarian intentions in posting political content that aligns with the Party-State's narratives, such as patriotism. For many fans, participation in nationalist actions is not indicative of genuine ideological alignment but rather a performative gesture to achieve mainstream recognition and acceptance of idol and fan culture. This performative engagement signifies a desire to reshape public perceptions and contributes to a more positive image for themselves and their idols within a complex digital landscape.

In essence, performative patriotism is practiced by multi-stakeholders, and is a key component of fandom nationalism in China. It reflects a complex interplay of agency, identity negotiation, and cultural resistance in the entertainment industry that is structured by state power, platform logic, and the economy of visibility. By critically examining the motivations and strategies employed by fans in response to political controversies, we can achieve a more nuanced insight into the transformative potential of performative practices and their capacity to shape narratives and digital cultures, which extends beyond the discussion of ideological conformity and oppression-versus-resistance. Through these nuanced discussions and observations, the landscape of performative patriotism emerges as a dynamic terrain of interaction between fan communities, business interests, the nationalist public, and state power. It offers a vantage point to investigate the intricate dynamics of cultural production and resistance within contemporary digital contexts.

Conclusion

By reviewing a wide range of relevant literature and zooming in on our ethnographic research on the case study of Zhang Zhehan's cancellation, we present to you a nuanced and up-to-date framework to understand stakeholders, practices, as well as power relations in fandom nationalism as a form of contemporary fan mobilization. Building on previous scholars' discussions on fandom nationalism, we differentiate between fan communities and nationalist citizens, and also include commercial stakeholders in consideration as another powerful stakeholder in addition to state institutions. This multi-stakeholder approach allows us to disentangle the complex interactions and power relations in the seemingly straightforward phenomenon of fan mobilization. Fandom nationalism as a phenomenon has become more routine in the Chinese and East Asian public sphere and has developed more complex dynamics when compared to its previous conceptualization. We argue that this complexity can be understood mainly through two concepts: participatory censorship and performative patriotism. Both concepts discuss not only the practices but also the dynamics between the involved stakeholders.

We adopt the concept of participatory censorship to highlight the self-organized fan practices, such as accusatory reporting, and the relationship between citizens and the Party-State in fandom nationalism. These fan practices on the one hand demonstrate fans' agency in mobilizing fan communities and citizens, yet are unquestionably structured by the state power and narrative on the other hand. Unlike the common scholarly narrative that Chinese fans are taken advantage of by the Party-State, the exploitation is mutual. The nationalist narratives and the anger of nationalist citizens have proven to be sharp and effective weapons to defeat rivals in fan wars and ruin celebrities' careers, which leads to the normalization of accusing the targeted celebrities of having problematic political stances with the intention to mobilize the citizens, businesses, and ultimately the Party-State to boycott or ban the celebrities. Zhang's cancellation illustrates the effectiveness of such a strategy and thus sets a very dangerous example: more extremist fans came to realize that finding or planting evidence of celebrities' betrayal of the nation is the easiest way to drag them and their fandom down. This makes Zhang's incident an even more egregious and horrific development of fandom nationalism.

We then turn to the concept of performative patriotism to bring out the crucial role of business interests in fandom nationalism, and to emphasize the performative nature of practices such as brands' termination announcements and fans' self-organized bans on entertainment-related posts on significant national dates. Structured by the visibility logic of social media platforms, both fans and businesses frequently display their patriotism via these practices, often insincerely, for social or economic capital gains. Since Zhang's cancellation, such performative patriotism practices are constantly conducted by not only fans but also celebrities who desire the vast Chinese market, practices that include self-censorship and ritualistic (re)posting of patriotic content on social media platforms. As the benefits of performing patriotism in China are increasingly evident, mobilizing and participating in nationalist collective actions becomes a common strategy in Chinese cultural industries and fandom.

There are two major structural powers in Chinese fandom nationalism as discussed in our case study: the Party-State and the social media platform Weibo. Even though we emphasize fans' agency in this process, these two stakeholders' structural powers should not be ignored. The idol fan communities mostly consist of young women, who already have a relatively disadvantaged social position in a patriarchal society. When facing accusations and attacks from mainstream society, conventional resistance often means paying a hefty price, such as having their fan accounts banned. Such power is sometimes even extended to neutral social media users who question cyberbullying and the censorship that targets victimized celebrities. Therefore, to avoid attacks from mainstream society and to keep themselves safe, fan communities choose silence or co-opt nationalist sentiments as an amulet for the fandoms and their idols to survive and thrive.

Integrating the two concepts mentioned above, we present to you a nuanced understanding of fandom nationalism in China. It is a set of practices that takes place in an intricate dynamic between multi-stakeholders in fandom. We define it as fandom-related individuals' or entities' voluntary and performative participatory practices that demonstrate state-endorsed patriotism/nationalism for control and/or for capital gains. It is structured by both the state's political power and the platforms' affordances and visibility logic. As you can see in our model illustrated in Figure 0.4, fandom nationalism in China, demonstrated by Zhang's cancellation, involves five main stakeholders: fan communities, nationalist citizens, businesses, social media platforms, and the Party-State. The latter two stakeholders (the outer circles in the model) function at the structural level in fandom nationalism, enabling and restricting other stakeholders' narratives and practices. The Party-State has unchallenged political power in the form of legal and political frameworks, and dominates the mainstream ideologies (e.g., nationalism) and norms (e.g., distrust in pop idol fandom culture) in Chinese society. Social media platforms' features and visibility logic afford and encourage fan collective practices, yet also censor them when deemed necessary. Under such structural powers, the other three stakeholders—fan communities, citizens, and businesses—all strategically align with the nationalist ideology in their practices, which undoubtedly further strengthen nationalist sentiments and narratives in Chinese society. Among these three stakeholders, nationalist citizens demonstrate less agency. Their nationalist sentiments can be exploited by anti-fans to attack targeted idols, as well as by businesses to profit from increased consumption or social media engagement. Fan communities' practices demonstrate the most complexity: their participatory censorship (e.g., accusatory reporting, comments management) constitutes a mutual exploitation relationship with the Party-State, and their performative patriotism sometimes serves as a subtle resistance to the structural powers while aligning and strengthening these powers.

This primer explains how fans' participatory censorship exposes their agency in utilizing the censorship system as a weapon for fan conflicts, but at the same time illustrates their internalization of the censorship ideology through interpretive labor. Driven by performative patriotism, the act of participatory censorship reveals that fans' engagements with nationalist actions are both performative and self-interested and closely related to their desire to gain acceptance from mainstream society. Yet, this process ironically assists the reinforcement of mainstream ideology and state propaganda. This duality highlights the framework of "governed/ungovernable." Fans' deep-seated affection and loyalty for their idols compel them to navigate and, at times, subvert the very structures that seek to control them, but at the same time, fans' behaviors and ideologies are inevitably shaped by these power structures.

The intersection of fan culture with broader societal narratives in contemporary China—East Asia in general too—illustrates a nuanced landscape of cultural expression, negotiation, and resistance. Within this context, participatory fandom practices serve as a microcosm of Chinese youth culture, encapsulating both the spirit of defiance against the mainstream social norms and the negotiation of adapting to existing sociopolitical constraints. These practices reflect young individuals' capacity to creatively engage with and challenge the constraints imposed by state governance, media platforms, and business exploitation. Through their participation, fans negotiate their identities, navigate societal expectations, and sometimes subvert mainstream patriarchal norms, highlighting their agility in maneuvering within a complex sociopolitical economic environment. This engagement not only reaffirms their agency and proactivity but also creatively redefines the boundaries of permissible expression within China's tightly controlled public sphere. Additionally, this vibrant interaction within fan communities underscores the evolving dialogue between traditional cultural values and modern expressions of identity, marking a significant shift in how youth culture manifests and influences the broader cultural landscape. Through these collective experiences, fans not only carve out spaces for personal and communal expression but also impact broader cultural, economic, and political discussions, demonstrating the profound influence of fandom in contemporary societal dynamics.

In China, idol fandom can be treated as an epitome of the Chinese youth culture and thus studying fandom is a significant way to understand the interactions between Chinese youth culture, media industry, and the Party-State. The current literature reveals a rich tapestry of how fandom interacts with political and ideological forces within China's digital landscape. Researchers like Song (2023); Liao, Koo, and Rojas (2022); and Fung (2009, 2013) have effectively mapped the terrain where fandom meets state governance and ideology, showing how these interactions shape fan practices and cultural impacts. This primer joins this dialogue by positioning fandom as a dynamic player in the broader discourse of youth culture and state interaction. We extend these discussions by delving deeper into how fandom acts not only as a field of cultural participation and consumption but also as a site of complex negotiations between personal agency and overarching state governance and ideologies. This also further explores the nuanced ways in which young people in China creatively subvert and utilize state ideologies and censorship to construct their own spaces for self-interest, resistance, and negotiation. Fandom in China has become a dynamic space where cultural expression intersects with the broader sociopolitical context. Within China's highly regulated media landscape, characterized by censorship and state control, fandom emerges as a site of contestation and negotiation where young individuals navigate and respond to political constraints.

Fandom not only acts as a stage for youth expression and resistance against authoritarian governance but also vividly mirrors the broader dynamics of youth culture in China. Young people utilize fandom as a medium to deploy creative strategies for youth expression and resistance against authoritarian governance and ideological control, such as coded language and symbolic gestures, to evade censorship and challenge prevailing political narratives. The use of homophonic replacements and slang words in online discourse reflects young people's ingenuity in subverting censorship measures, demonstrating a form of resistance against state restrictions on free speech and expression. Simultaneously, the way Chinese youth navigate the complexities of censorship and political sensitivities illustrates their sophisticated understanding of and engagement with the sociopolitical environment. Their participation in fandom nationalist actions, often characterized by performative patriotism, is not just an endorsement of state narratives but a nuanced strategy to negotiate social acceptance and affirm their identities within tightly controlled societal structures. This dual approach—resisting suppression while adapting to it—underscores the complex agency of Chinese youth. Fandom, therefore, provides a critical lens through which to observe the negotiation of identity, values, and community among young people, making it a definitive microcosm of contemporary Chinese youth culture. The role of fan culture as an epitome of Chinese youth culture underscores its capacity to challenge and accommodate censorship and suppression simultaneously, showcasing the dynamic agency of young individuals in negotiating political realities while asserting cultural identities within a highly controlled media environment. This nuanced perspective enriches our understanding of how cultural practices intersect with politics, shaping the landscape of contemporary youth culture in China.

While we develop the conceptualization and the model based on Zhang's case and the Chinese sociopolitical context, we believe in their capacity to shed light on broader fandom participatory practices formed under various forms of structural power. Our multi-stakeholder perspective paints a more intricate network that goes beyond the dichotomy between oppression versus resistance, and agency versus exploitation. The concept of participatory censorship can also provide a non-normative framework to understand the phenomenon of cancel culture and its manifestations across cultural contexts. Together with previous literature on performative allyship and activism, our exploration of performative patriotism reveals the importance of studying the more insincere and performative forms of fan practices.

We also intend to contribute to fan studies methodologically with this primer. In recent years, a significant trend has emerged in both Chinese and Western academia, wherein fan studies are increasingly being conducted through the lens of digital ethnography. This is largely attributed to the growing reliance of fan activities on virtual interactions, which requires researchers to delve into the realm of internet-based fan culture (Booth and Williams 2021). However, we believe that a considerable portion of studies purporting to employ digital ethnography might lack rigor and potentially would benefit from including on-the-ground ethnography. Merely selecting a handful of comments on platforms and screenshots based on short-period observation is insufficient and can cause researchers' omission of hidden patterns. The crux of digital ethnography lies in a prolonged and immersive participant observation (Wang and Liu 2021). The absence of such sustained immersion hinders researchers from comprehensively understanding fandom as a cultural phenomenon from the participants' perspectives, subsequently impeding the grasp of fans' positions and interpretations. This deficiency often leads to misconceptions, as well as overly simplified analyses of fan culture. Consequently, relying solely on social media posts as a case study presents an unbalanced and oversimplified representation. As Hills (2017) critiques, some studies that assert themselves as digital ethnographies lack substantial fieldwork materials. Adopting a purely virtual approach, where scholars sit behind a computer screen and type away, is, in essence, a form of intellectual complacency. This choice may stem from the convenience it offers rather than inherent scholarly rigor. Given that fans' online expressions are intricately tied to their real-world identities and social status, an examination of fan practices that isolates either the digital or the physical realm risks falling into a dualistic framework. Hills (2017) aptly posits that digital fandom represents a hybridized form of engagement, as fans aspire to transcend incessant mediation and attain the co-presence inherent in physical conventions. Ethnographic research requires repeated forays into people's lives (Ingold 2014), and it stands to reason that people's lives are hybrid, a mix of digital practices and activities in the physical world.

Through a long-term immersive ethnographic investigation, our research breaks down the stereotypical binary of online and offline division of fan culture and sees fan practices as a hybrid and dynamic whole. This is also why we choose to combine digital and on-the-ground ethnography: it does not mechanically categorize fan practices into two distinct realms of online and offline. Conversely, our primary focus is on the same group of fan informants, primarily composed of twenty-five individuals, and how their digital activities and physical practices have evolved and diverged. We explore the factors influencing these changes, as well as the informants' perceptions of their evolving practices during that period. The varying manifestations of digital and physical practices are shaped by diverse political, socio-economic, and cultural contexts, as well as the profound influence of technological and media interfaces. The methodology employed in this research represents a pioneering attempt at using a mixed ethnographic approach of both digital ethnography and multi-sited fieldwork. As the digital fandom landscape continues to evolve, it becomes increasingly imperative for future research to adopt methodologies that mirror the complex interplay between digital and physical realms.

We hope this primer has not only helped your understanding of the intricate dynamics between fandom and nationalism in China and East Asia in general but also demonstrated to you how to conduct quality ethnographic research in a contemporary digitized society and fandom culture.

APPENDIX I
FAN INFORMANTS LIST

The following table records the basic profile of these twenty-five informants: "First acquaintance" shows how we first became acquainted with them. Some were fan friends we had met before or during the digital ethnography, and our friendship developed from the digital world to real life, where they eventually became my informants and introduced me to some of their own friends. We got to know a few informants, such as Bella and Dora, through such introductions. Similarly, another category of informants is those whom we became acquainted with during the on-the-ground ethnography, for example, Celia and Gill, who we kept in touch with after the fan events and who eventually became my long-term informants.

Under the column "In-person meeting," we indicated the cities in which we participated in informants' fan-centric events, encompassing fan gatherings, concerts, birthday celebrations, and comic markets. Our interactions with the informants extended far beyond interviews, contributing to a multifaceted understanding of fandom, fan culture, and fan practices. Given the ethos of our ethnography as a testament to sustained participant observation, our involvement in informants' fan activities spanned multiple occasions and encompassed a diverse array of events to obtain a comprehensive dataset.

TABLE 2 Anonymous Informants' Information

Anon. ID	Birth year	Sex	First acquaintance	First chat/interview	In-person meeting	Frequency of information updates
01 Abby	1998	F	Weibo	Dec 27, 2020 Fans gathering, Tianjin	Guangzhou, Suzhou, Tianjin	March, May 2021
02 Bella	2000	F	Abby's friend	Nov 12, 2021 Video recording	No	No
03 Celia	1996	F	Concert in Guangzhou	Dec 27, 2020 Fans gathering and in-person interview, Guangzhou	Guangzhou, Suzhou	May 2021
04 Dora	1999	F	Abby's friend	May 4, 2021 Fans gathering, Suzhou	Suzhou, Shanghai	June, August 2021

Anon. ID	Birth year	Sex	First acquaintance	First chat/interview	In-person meeting	Frequency of information updates
05 Elly	1997	F	Weibo	May 4, 2021 Casual dialogue before concert, Suzhou	Suzhou	September 2021
06 Flora	1995	F	Weibo	Jan 10, 2021 Video interview on WeChat	Hengdian	September 2021
07 Gill	1995	F	Concert in Guangzhou	May 13, 2021 In-person interview, Suzhou	Changsha	March 2021
08 Hailey	1997	F	Weibo	May 4, 2021 In-person interview, Suzhou	Suzhou, Changsha	September 2021
09 Iris	1992	F	Weibo	Dec 13, 2020 Fans gathering, Tianjin	Beijing, Tianjin, Suzhou	December 2020, September 2021

Anon. ID	Birth year	Sex	First acquaintance	First chat/interview	In-person meeting	Frequency of information updates
10 Jenny	1997	F	Iris's friend	June 12, 2021 Video interview on WeChat	No	August 2021
11 Karen	1998	F	Elly's friend	July 23, 2021 Video interview on WeChat	No	March 2021
12 Lily	2000	F	Flora's friend	Dec 20, 2020 Fans gathering, Beijing	Beijing, Shanghai	July, September 2021
13 Meg	2000	F	Weibo	Aug 20, 2020 Telephone interview	Tianjin, Hengdian	July, August 2021
14 Nina	1996	F	Meg's friend	June 12, 2021 Video interview on WeChat	Shanghai, Hengdian	September 2021

Anon. ID	Birth year	Sex	First acquaintance	First chat/interview	In-person meeting	Frequency of information updates
15 Ole	1997	F	Iris's friend	Sep 13, 2021 Telephone interview	Suzhou	September 2021
16 Penny	1995	F	Weibo	Dec 20, 2020 Fans gathering, Beijing	No	October 2021
17 Quella	1991	F	Celia's friend	Dec 20, 2020 Fans gathering, Beijing	Guangzhou	December 2020
18 Rose	1985	F	Weibo	June 29, 2021 In-person interview, Shanghai	Shanghai	October, November 2021
19 Silvia	1980	F	Rose's friend	March 27, 2021 Telephone interview	No	July 2021

Anon. ID	Birth year	Sex	First acquaintance	First chat/interview	In-person meeting	Frequency of information updates
20 Tina	1983	F	WeChat group A	March 15, 2021 WeChat group chat	Changsha	October 2021
21 Vera	1993	F	Rose's friend	March 15, 2021 WeChat group chat	No	March 2021
22 Wendy	2001	F	Concert in Tianjin	July 21, 2021 Video interview on WeChat	Changsha, Guangzhou	September, October 2021
23 Yumi	1985	F	WeChat group A	X month, In-person interview	Y City	X month
24 Zoe	1994	F	Weibo	April 23, 2021 WeChat video interview	No	November 17, 2021
25 Xenia	1992	F	Weibo	September 8, 2021 Fans gathering (Hengdian)	Hengdian	September 15, 2021

The "Frequency of informant updates" column encapsulates the dates when additional interactions were conducted beyond the initial one. These engagements encompassed supplementary interviews, casual conversations during fan gatherings, and face-to-face interactions at fan events such as concerts. Throughout the research timeline, we maintained continuous communication, engaging with informants to observe their evolving fan experiences and reflections, particularly during Zhang's case.

APPENDIX II
ABBREVIATIONS AND GLOSSARIES

This list encompasses the key internet slang, fandom jargon, and coded language commonly used within the Chinese fan culture that are referenced throughout this book, including the frequently occurring specialized abbreviations.

TABLE 3 List of Abbreviations and Glossaries

being cold	凉了 is an internet slang in Chinese fandom, meaning that a person's body turns cold after death, a metaphor for a celebrity's career being completely ruined.
BL	"Boys' Love," originated as a genre of Japanese manga in the 1970s, featuring "love, sex and romance between boys and young men," and has been translated into different forms of cultural texts (Martin 2012, 365).
CAC	中华人民共和国国家互联网信息办公室, the Cyberspace Administration of China
CAPA	Chinese Performing Arts Association
CCDI	Central Commission for Discipline Inspection

CP-fan	A community of fans who celebrate and fantasize about a romantic relationship between their favorite characters or actors.
cutting leeks	割韭菜 is a common term in Chinese internet slang to describe marketing practices that focus on short-term profits without a long-term development plan. Because leeks are a very hardy vegetable, when the leaves are cut off from the root and sold, they will soon grow back. Just like a steady stream of fans from one generation to the next, sponsors invite the popular stars to endorse their products, thinking only about how they can drain the fans' pockets of every penny in the short term, without any thought of developing long-term loyal customers. The financial situation and sustainability of the fans are not respected.
eat melon	吃瓜 is a Chinese internet slang for bystanders watching the hilarity.
eating sweets	嗑糖 is a commonly used jargon among CP-fans, which signifies the act of deriving implicit romantic cues from the interactions between the idols being paired.
gege	"哥哥," in Chinese, the term is the same as "brother," but it serves as an affectionate form of address used by fans for their male idols and does not imply any familial relationship. This is also the reason we use "gege" in the quotations directly.
house collapsed	塌房, a fan-made internet slang, refers to an idol having scandals and ruining their career.
Kongping	控评 means controlling comments. It is one of the most important fans' daily tasks to keep the comments positive under the posts related to their idols.

making data	做数据, an important component of fans' daily tasks, involves extensive data labor (Yin 2020) on social media to increase their idols' shares, comments, and likes. This effort aims to cultivate a positive online image and high popularity for the idols, ultimately seeking to secure more sponsorships and job opportunities for them.
moneymaker daddy	金主爸爸, a fan-made internet slang, refers to the sponsors and investors.
no idols before the state	国家面前无偶像 is a popular slogan frequently used by Chinese fans to demonstrate that, when faced with conflicting positions between the state and their idols, the state is regarded as the singular priority.
NRTA	National Radio Television Administration
popular comments	热门评论 is an important feature on Weibo, which highlights and shows the comments with the most likes at the top of the comments section under posts.
Qinglang Campaign/ Sweep-up Campaign	清朗行动, in June 2021, the Cyberspace Administration of China began the *Qinglang Campaign* [清朗行动], targeting online fan communities in China with the goal to clean up harmful collective actions in fandoms, such as fan wars and fan conflicts on various levels.
selling *fu*	卖腐 is a fan-made slang similar to queerbaiting, which means making the homosexual elements as selling points.
The Untamed	陈情令, *Chen qing ling*, is a BL-adapted drama produced by Tencent and aired in 2019. The protagonists are Xiao Zhan and Wang Yibo.

The Word of Honor	山河令, *Shan he ling*, is a BL-adapted drama produced by Youku and aired in 2021. The protagonists are Gong Jun and Zhang Zhehan.
worshipping the devil	拜鬼, every year, on the anniversary of Japan's surrender in the Second World War, Japanese politicians or celebrities usually visit the Yasukuni Shrine, which is strongly protested and condemned by the Chinese government and the public as "worshipping the devil."

AUTHORS' BIOGRAPHIES

Erika Ningxin Wang (PhD, King's College London) is an assistant professor at The Chinese University of Hong Kong, Shenzhen. Erika's research interests lie at the intersection of youth culture, digital media, and state governance. She has been elected as the Early Career Representative of the International Communication Association, Division of Popular Media and Culture. Her recent publications in fan studies appear in *Social Media+Society*, *Asian Studies Review*, *Communication Culture and Critique*, and *Celebrity Studies*.

Qian Huang (PhD, Erasmus University Rotterdam) is an assistant professor of digital cultures at the University of Groningen in the Netherlands. She has published articles on Chinese digital vigilantism, digital visibility, cancel culture in fandom, and nationalism in China in peer-reviewed journals such as *International Journal of Cultural Studies*, *Social Media+Society*, and *International Journal of Communication*. She is also a co-author of the book *Digital Media, Denunciation and Shaming: The Court of Public Opinion*, and a co-editor of the volume *Introducing Vigilant Audiences*.

BIBLIOGRAPHY

Abidin, Crystal. 2019. "Yes Homo: Gay Influencers, Homonormativity, and Queerbaiting on YouTube." *Continuum* 33 (5): 614–29. https://doi.org/10.1080/10304312.2019.1644806.

Anderson, Benedict. 2006. *Imagined Communities: Reflections on the Origin and Spread of Nationalism*. Verso.

Banet-Weiser, Sara. 2018. *Empowered: Popular Feminism and Popular Misogyny*. Duke University Press.

Billig, Michael. 2005. *Banal Nationalism*. Sage.

Blair, Kelsey. 2021. "Empty Gestures: Performative Utterances and Allyship." *Journal of Dramatic Theory and Criticism* 35 (2): 53–73.

Booth, Paul. 2015. *Playing Fans: Negotiating Fandom and Media in the Digital Age*. University of Iowa Press.

Booth, Paul. 2017. *Digital Fandom 2.0* [online]. Available from: https://www.peterlang.com/document/1054582. Accessed March 14, 2022.

Booth, Paul, and Rebecca Williams. 2021. *A Fan Studies Primer*: *Method, Research, Ethics*. University of Iowa Press.

Bouvier, Gwen. 2020. "Racist Call-Outs and Cancel Culture on Twitter: The Limitations of the Platform's Ability to Define Issues of Social Justice." *Discourse, Context & Media* 38: 100431. https://doi.org/10.1016/j.dcm.2020.100431.

Brennan, Joseph. 2018. "Queerbaiting: The 'Playful' Possibilities of Homoeroticism." *International Journal of Cultural Studies* 21 (2): 189–206. https://doi.org/10.1177/1367877916631050.

CAC (Cyberspace Administration of China). 2016. "The Cyber Administration of China Led the 'Sweep-up' Series of Campaigns in 2016 国家网信办牵头开展清朗系列专项行动." http://www.cac.gov.cn/2016-11/25/c_1119991081.htm.

CAC (Cyberspace Administration of China). 2021a. "The Cyberspace Administration of China Begins Clearing Up the Chaos in Fandom Campaign 中央网信办启动'清朗饭圈'乱象整治专项行动." http://www.cac.gov.cn/2021-06/08/c_1624735580427196.htm. Accessed October 29, 2021.

CAC (Cyberspace Administration of China). 2021b. "Notice on Further Regulating the Chaos in Fandom 关于加强饭圈乱象治理的通知." http://www.cac.gov.cn/2021-08/26/c_1631563902354584.html. Accessed October 29, 2021.

Cai, Shenshen. 2016. *State Propaganda in China's Entertainment Industry*. Routledge.

Chen, Dan, and Gengsong Gao. 2023. "Chinese Celebrities' Political Signalling on Sina Weibo." *The China Quarterly* 254: 466–83. https://doi.org/10.1017/S0305741022001734.

Chen, Lu. 2017. "The Emergence of the Anti-Hallyu Movement in China." *Media, Culture & Society* 39 (3): 374–90. https://doi.org/10.1177/0163443716646176.

Chew, Matthew M. 2023. "Cybernationalist Authoritarianism: Fangirls' Peer Production of the Virtual Celebrity 'Oppa China'." *China Information* 37 (1): 75–99. https://doi.org/10.1177/0920203X231156357.

Chin, Bertha, and Lori Morimoto. 2013. "Towards a Theory of Transcultural Fandom." *Participations: Journal of Audience & Reception Studies* 10 (1): 92–108. https://doi.org/10.17613/M6RP98.

Clark, Meredith D. 2020. "DRAG THEM: A Brief Etymology of So-Called 'Cancel Culture'." *Communication and the Public* 5 (3–4): 88–92. https://doi.org/10.1177/2057047320961562.

Cole, Michael. 2024. "The Evolution of Ukrainian Football Ultras in the Context of War: Tribune of Heroes." In *Football, Fandom and Collective Memory*, edited by Przemysław Nosal, Radosław Kossakowski, and Wojciech Woźniak, 15–32. Routledge.

Communist Youth League of China. 2021. "Communist Youth League of China: The 'Business of Patriotism' Needs to Stop 共青团中央：'爱国生意'当休矣." *news.ifeng.com*, September 29, 2021. https://news.ifeng.com/c/89vLkTRiq79.

Cui, Di, and Fang Wu. 2024. "Toward an Operationality Perspective on Fandom: Exploring Chinese Fans' Emerging Practices in Platform-Mediated Environments." *New Media & Society* 0 (0). https://doi.org/10.1177/14614448241249134.

Cui, Jie. 2025. "We Are Citizens, Not Fans': Frictions and Negotiations in Idolizing the Nation in State Propaganda." *Asian Journal of Communication* 35 (1): 58–76. https://doi.org/10.1080/01292986.2024.2420273.

Dahlberg, Lincoln. 2007. "Rethinking the Fragmentation of the Cyberpublic: From Consensus to Contestation." *New Media & Society* 9 (5): 827–47. https://doi.org/10.1177/1461444807081228.

Devlin, Michael B., Kenon A. Brown, Natalie Brown-Devlin, and Andrew C. Billings. 2020. "'My Country Is Better than Yours': Delineating Differences between Six Countries' National Identity, Fan Identity, and Media Consumption during the 2018 Olympic Games." *Sociology of Sports Journal* 37 (3): 254–63. https://doi.org/10.1123/ssj.2019-0125.

Dong, Yujie, Yuheng Wu, Fang Wu, Yi Mou, and Alex Ivanov. 2022. "From Homeland-Mother to Azhong-Brother: A Qualitative Study of Nation Anthropomorphism among Chinese Youths." *Media, Culture & Society* 44 (7): 1354–71. https://doi.org/10.1177/01634437221104692.

Downey, John, and Natalie Fenton. 2003. "New Media, Counter Publicity and the Public Sphere." *New Media & Society* 5 (2): 185–202. https://doi.org/10.1177/1461444803005002003.

Dutton, Michael. 2008. "Passionately Governmental: Maoism and the Structured Intensities of Revolutionary Governmentality." *Postcolonial Studies* 11 (1): 303–14. https://doi.org/10.1080/13688790801971563.

Fang, Kecheng, and Maria Repnikova. 2018. "Demystifying 'Little Pink': The Creation and Evolution of a Gendered Label for Nationalistic Activists in China." *New Media & Society* 20 (6): 2162–85. https://doi.org/10.1177/1461444817731923.

Fraser, Nancy. 1990. "Rethinking the Public Sphere: A Contribution to the Critique of Actually Existing Democracy." *Social Text* (25/26): 56–80. https://doi.org/10.2307/466240.

Freshwater, Helen. 2004. "Towards a Redefinition of Censorship." In *Censorship & Cultural Regulation in the Modern Age*, edited by Beate Müller, 217–37. Brill. https://doi.org/10.1163/9789401200950_010.

Fung, Anthony Y. H. 2009. "Fandom, Youth and Consumption in China." *European Journal of Cultural Studies* 12 (3): 285–303. https://doi.org/10.1177/1367549409105365.

Fung, Anthony Y. H. 2013. "Deliberating Fandom and the New Wave of Chinese Pop: A Case Study of Chris Li." *Popular Music* 32 (1): 79–89. https://doi.org/10.1017/S0261143012000566.

Fung, Anthony Y. H. 2019. "Fandomization of Online Video or Television in China." *Media, Culture & Society* 41 (7): 995–1010. https://doi.org/10.1177/0163443719863353.

Gao, Gengsong, and Dan Chen. 2024. "Fan Engagement with Chinese Celebrities' Political Signaling on Weibo." *Journal of Contemporary China* (August): 1–21. https://doi.org/10.1080/10 670564.2024.2389249.

Goffman, Ervin. 2023. "The Presentation of Self in Everyday Life." In *Social Theory Re-wired*, edited by Wesley Longhofer and Daniel Winchester, 482–93. Routledge.

Gong, Yuan. 2022. "Transcultural Taste and Neoliberal Patriotic Subject: A Study of Chinese Fans' Online Talk of K-Pop." *Poetics* 93 (August): 101665. https://doi.org/10.1016/j. poetic.2022.101665.

Gries, Peter Hays. 2007. "Narratives to Live By: The Century of Humiliation and Chinese National Identity Today." In *China's Transformations: The Stories beyond the Headlines*, edited by Lionel M. Jensen and Timothy B. Weston, 112–28. Rowman & Littlefield.

Guan, Tianru, and Tingting Hu. 2020. "The Conformation and Negotiation of Nationalism in China's Political Animations—A Case Study of Year Hare Affair." *Continuum* 34 (3): 417–30. https://doi.org/10.1080/10304312.2020.1724882.

Guo, Shaohua. 2023. "Tracing the Bunny: Animating Propaganda Work Online." *Journal of Asian Studies* 82 (3): 407–26. https:// doi.org/10.1215/00219118-10471981.

Han, Gil-Soo. 2015. "K-Pop Nationalism: Celebrities and Acting Blackface in the Korean Media." *Continuum* 29 (1): 2–16. https:// doi.org/10.1080/10304312.2014.968522.

Han, Rongbin. 2015. "Defending the Authoritarian Regime Online: China's 'Voluntary Fifty-Cents Army'." *The China Quarterly* 224: 1006–25. https://doi.org/10.1017/S0305741015001216.

Han, Rongbin. 2021. "Cyber Nationalism and Regime Support under Xi Jinping: The Effects of the 2018 Constitutional Revision." *Journal of Contemporary China* 30 (131): 717–33. https://doi.org/10.1080/10670564.2021.1884957.

He, Qijun, and Yungeng Li. 2023. "Civic Engagement Intention and the Data-Driven Fan Community: Investigating the Motivation behind Chinese Fans' Online Data-Making Behavior from a Collective Action Perspective." *Social Media + Society* 9 (1): 1–16. https://doi.org/10.1177/20563051221150409.

Hills, Matt. 2013. "Fiske's 'Textual Productivity' and Digital Fandom: Web 2.0 Democratization versus Fan Distinction." *Participations: Journal of Audience & Reception Studies* 10 (1): 130–53.

Hills, Matt. 2017. "Foreword." In *Digital Fandom 2.0. New Media Studies*, edited by Paul Booth. Peter Lang Verlag. https://doi.org/10.3726/978-1-4539-1654-4.

Hu, Tingting, and Cathy Yue Wang. 2021. "Who Is the Counterpublic? Bromance-as-masquerade in Chinese Online Drama—SCI Mystery." *Television & New Media* 22 (6): 671–86. https://doi.org/10.1177/1527476420937262.

Hu, Tingting, Liang Ge, Ziyao Chen, and Xu Xia. 2024a. "Masculinity in Crisis? Reticent/han-xu Politics against Danmei and Male Effeminacy." *International Journal of Cultural Studies* 26 (3): 274–92. https://doi.org/10.1177/13678779231159424.

Hu, Tingting, Liang Ge, and Cathy Yue Wang. 2024b. "A State against Boys' Love? Reviewing the Trajectory of Censorship over Danmei." *Continuum* 38 (2): 229–38. https://doi.org/10.1080/10304312.2024.2357335.

Huang, Haiyan, and Lutgard Lams. 2024. "'Together, We Achieve the China Dream': Constructing Affective Chinese Nationalities in the Film My People, My Country." *Journal of Current Chinese Affairs* 54 (1): 73–93. https://doi.org/10.1177/18681026241239976.

Huang, Qian. 2023. "The Discursive Construction of Populist and Misogynist Nationalism: Digital Vigilantism against Unpatriotic Intellectual Women in China." *Social Media + Society* 9 (2): 1–13. https://doi.org/10.1177/20563051231170816.

Huang, Qian, and Alice Janssens. 2019. "Come Mangiare un Cannolo con Le Bacchette: The Contested Field of Luxury Fashion in China, A Case Study of the 2018 Dolce & Gabbana Advertising Incident." *ZoneModa Journal* 9 (2): 123–40. https://doi.org/10.6092/issn.2611-0563/9970.

Huang, Qian, Simone Driessen, and Daniel Trottier. 2023. "When Pop and Politics Collide: A Transcultural Perspective on Contested Practices in Pop Idol Fandoms in China and the West." *International Journal of Communication* 17 (February): 1425–44. https://ijoc.org/index.php/ijoc/article/view/17255/4061.

Huat, Chua Beng. 2004. "Conceptualizing an East Asian Popular Culture." *Inter-Asia Cultural Studies* 5 (2): 200–21. https://doi.org/10.1080/1464937042000236711.

Ifeng. 2021. *Zhang Zhehan Has Lost All His Endorsements! More than 26 Brands Have Announced the Termination of their*

Contracts. Assessed September 29, 2021. https://ent.ifeng. com/c/88fnXtl9zmM.

Ingold, Tim. 2014. "That's Enough about Ethnography!" *HAU: Journal of Ethnographic Theory* 4 (1): 383–95. http://dx.doi. org/10.14318/hau4.1.021.

Iwabuchi, Koichi. 2002. *Recentering Globalization: Popular Culture and Japanese Transnationalism*. Duke University Press. https://doi.org/10.1215/9780822384083.

Jansen, Sue Curry. 1988. *Censorship: The Knot That Binds Power and Knowledge*. Oxford University Press.

Jenkins, Henry. 1992. *Textual Poachers: Television Fans and Participatory Cultures*. Routledge.

Jenkins, Henry. 2006. *Convergence Culture: Where Old and New Media Collide*. New York University Press.

Jenkins, Henry. 2009. *Confronting the Challenges of Participatory Culture: Media Education for the 21st Century*. MIT Press.

Jenkins, Henry. 2020. "An Archive Not of Their Own: Fan Fiction & Controversy in China." http://henryjenkins.org/blog/2020/3/24/ an-archive-not-of-their-own-fan-fiction-controversy-in-china.

Jin, Dal Yong. 2021. "The BTS Sphere: Adorable Representative M.C. for Youth's Transnational Cyber-Nationalism on Social Media." *Communication and the Public* 6 (1–4): 33–47. https:// doi.org/10.1177/20570473211046733.

Johnston, Hank. 2024. "The MAGA Movement's Big Umbrella." *Mobilization: An International Quarterly* 28 (4): 409–33. https://doi.org/10.17813/1086-671X-28-4-409.

Joo, Jeongsuk. 2011. "Transnationalization of Korean Popular Culture and the Rise of 'Pop Nationalism' in Korea." *The Journal of Popular Culture* 44 (3): 489–504. https://doi. org/10.1111/j.1540-5931.2011.00845.x.

Kang, Jennifer M. 2023. "The Politics of Being a K-Pop Fan: Korean Fandom and the 'Cancel the Japan Tour' Protest." *International Journal of Communication* 17 (January): 1019–37. https://ijoc.org/index.php/ijoc/article/view/18885.

Kim, Jeongmee. 2007. "Why Does Hallyu Matter? The Significance of the Korean Wave in South Korea." *Critical Studies in Television* 2 (2): 47–59. https://doi.org/10.7227/CST.2.2.6.

Kim, Youna. 2022. "Soft Power and Cultural Nationalism: Globalization of the Korean Wave." In *Media in Asia: Global, Digital, Gendered and Mobile*, edited by Youna Kim, 93–106. Routledge.

Kottak, Conrad P. 2002. *Anthropology: The Exploration of Human Diversity*. McGraw-Hill, Inc.

Lams, Lutgard, and Wendy Weile Zhou. 2023. "Pseudo-Participation, Authentic Nationalism: Understanding Chinese Fanquan Girls' Personifications of the Nation-State." *Asian Journal of Communication* 33 (1): 38–59. https://doi.org/10.1080/01292986.2022.2144919.

Lee, Jin, and Crystal Abidin. 2022. "Oegugin Influencers and Pop Nationalism through Government Campaigns: Regulating Foreign-Nationals in the South Korean YouTube Ecology." *Policy & Internet* 14 (3): 541–57. https://doi.org/10.1002/poi3.319.

Leung, Lisa Y. M. 2021. "Mediating Asian Modernities: The Lessons of Korean Dramas." In *The Soft Power of the Korean Wave*, edited by Youna Kim, 184–95. Routledge.

Leung, Lisa Y. M. 2023. "The 'Rational' Fan? Negotiating Transnational Cosmopolitanism and Nationalism among Hong Kong BTS Fans." *Inter-Asia Cultural Studies* 24 (5): 793–808. https://doi.org/10.1080/14649373.2023.2242144.

Liao, Xining. 2023. "From the Eyes of Censorship Supporters: Chinese Attitudes Regarding Two Types of Online Censorship." *Asian Journal of Communication* 33 (6): 611–30. https://doi.org/10.1080/01292986.2023.2253272.

Liao, Xining, Alex Zhi-Xiong Koo, and Hernando Rojas. 2022. "Fandom Nationalism in China: The Effects of Idol Adoration and Online Fan Community Engagement." *Chinese Journal of Communication* 15 (4): 558–81. https://doi.org/10.1080/17544750.2022.2088587.

Liu, Hailong, ed. 2019. *From Cyber-Nationalism to Fandom Nationalism: The Case of Diba Expedition in China*. Routledge. https://doi.org/10.4324/9780429447754.

Liu, Shih-Diing. 2006. "China's Popular Nationalism on the Internet. Report on the 2005 Anti-Japan Network Struggles." *Inter-Asia Cultural Studies* 7 (1): 144–55. https://doi.org/10.1080/14649370500463802.

Luo, Zhifan. 2024. "Negotiating Censorial Power and Its Legitimacy: A Case Study of the Second Face of State Censorship." *Journal of Political Power* 17 (2): 1–22. https://doi.org/10.1080/2158379X.2024.2370813.

Luo, Zhifan, and Li. Muya 2022. "Participatory Censorship: How Online Fandom Community Facilitates Authoritarian

Rule." *New Media & Society* 26 (7): 4236–54. https://doi. org/10.1177/14614448221113923.

Lyan, Irina. 2019. "Welcome to Korea Day: From Diasporic to Hallyu 'Fan-Nationalism'." *International Journal of Communication* 13 (August): 3764–80. https://ijoc.org/index. php/ijoc/article/view/11153.

Martin, Fran. 2012. "Girls Who Love Boys' Love: Japanese Homoerotic *Manga* as Trans-national Taiwan Culture." *Inter-Asia Cultural Studies* 13 (3): 365–83. https://doi.org/10.1080/146 49373.2012.689707.

Miller, Daniel. 2018. "Digital Anthropology." In *The Open Encyclopedia of Anthropology*, edited by Felix Stein. Facsimile of the first edition in *The Cambridge Encyclopedia of Anthropology*. Online: http://doi.org/10.29164/18digital.

Ng, Eve. 2020. "No Grand Pronouncements Here … : Reflections on Cancel Culture and Digital Media Participation." *Television & New Media* 21 (6): 621–7.

Ng, Eve. 2022. *Cancel Culture: A Critical Analysis*. Springer Nature.

Noonan, Patrick J. 2008. *Creating a Counterpublic: Terayama Shûji and Tenjô Sajiki's, Documentary Runaway (1969)*. University of California.

Norris, Pippa. 2023. "Cancel Culture: Myth or Reality?" *Political Studies* 71 (1): 145–74. https://doi. org/10.1177/00323217211037023.

Nosal, Przemysław, Radosław Kossakowski, and Wojciech Woźniak. 2021. "Guerrilla Patriotism and Mnemonic Wars: Cursed Soldiers as Role Models for Football Fans in Poland." *Sport in Society* 24 (11): 2050–65. https://doi.org/10.1080/17430437.202 1.1892644.

NRTA. 2021. "The General Office of the National Radio and Television Administration Notice on Further Strengthening the Management of Cultural Programs and Their Personnel国家广播电视总局办公厅关于进一步加强文艺节目及其人员管理的通知." http://www.nrta.gov.cn/art/2021/9/2/art_113_57756.html.

Ou, Chuyue, and Zhongxuan Lin. 2023. "Co-Presence, Dysco-Presence, and Disco-Presence: Navigating WeChat in Chinese Acquaintance Networks." *New Media & Society* 26 (12): 7236–54. https://doi.org/10.1177/14614448231168566.

Qin, Qin. 2022. "The Beijing Rainbow Film Festival: Between Depoliticisation and Performative Activism." *Culture, Health &*

Sexuality 24 (10): 1438–50. https://doi.org/10.1080/13691058.2021.1965218.

Quick, Kathryn S., and John M. Bryson. 2022. "Chapter 14: Public Participation." In *Handbook on Theories of Governance*, edited by Christopher Ansell and Jacob Torfing, 158–68. Edward Elgar Publishing. https://doi.org/10.4337/9781800371972.00022.

Richter, Andrei. 2008. "Post-Soviet Perspective on Censorship and Freedom of the Media: An Overview." *International Communication Gazette* 70 (5): 307–24. https://doi.org/10.1177/1748048508094291.

Rosaldo, Renato I. 1999. "A Note on Geertz as a Cultural Essayist." *Representation* 59 (1997): 30–4. https://doi.org/10.2307/2928813.

Schneider, Florian. 2016. "The Cultural Governance of Mass Media in Contemporary China." In *Handbook of Cultural and Creative Industries in China*, edited by Michael Keane, 189–206. Edward Elgar Publishing.

Schneider, Florian. 2018. *China's Digital Nationalism*. Oxford Studies in Digital Politics.

Schneider, Florian. 2021. "COVID-19 Nationalism and the Visual Construction of Sovereignty during China's Coronavirus Crisis." *China Information* 35 (3): 301–24. https://doi.org/10.1177/0920203X211034692.

Schneider, Florian. 2023. "China's Digital Nationalism." In *The Routledge Handbook of Nationalism in East and Southeast Asia*, edited by Zhouxiang Lu, 189–206. Routledge.

Shan, Wei, and Juan Chen. 2021. "The Little Pinks: Self-Mobilized Nationalism and State Allies in Chinese Cyberspace." *International Journal of China Studies* 12 (1): 25–46. https://jice.um.edu.my/index.php/IJCS/article/view/36670.

Shen, Cuihua, and He Gong. 2019. "Personal Ties, Group Ties and Latent Ties: Connecting Network Size to Diversity and Trust in the Mobile Social Network WeChat." *Asian Journal of Communication* 29 (1): 18–34. https://doi.org/10.1080/01292986.2018.1504976

Silverman, David. 2015. *Interpreting Qualitative Data*. Sage.

Sina, Weibo. 2015. *Weibo Announces First Quarter 2025 Unaudited Financial Results*. Sina Weibo. http://ir.weibo.com/news-releases/news-release-details/weibo-announces-first-quarter-2025-unaudited-financial-results.

Song, Chenyang. 2023. "Digital Truth-Making among the New Chinese Online Fandom Nationalists." December. https://doi.org/10.16995/ee.8970.

Song, Lin. 2023. "Politics of Fun and Participatory Censorship: China's Reception of Animal Crossing: New Horizons." *Convergence* 29 (6): 1453–64. https://doi.org/10.1177/13548565221117476.

Spielmann, Nathalie, Susan Dobscha, and L. J. Shrum. 2023. "Brands and Social Justice Movements: The Effects of True versus Performative Allyship on Brand Evaluation." *Journal of the Association for Consumer Research* 8 (1): 83–94. https://doi.org/10.1086/722697.

Stanfill, Mel. 2019. *Exploiting Fandom: How the Media Industry Seeks to Manipulate Fans*. University of Iowa Press.

Stanfill, Mel. 2020. "Introduction: The Reactionary in the Fan and the Fann in the Reactionary." *Television & New Media* 21 (2): 123–34. https://doi.org/10.1177/1527476419879912.

Stanfill, Mel. 2024. *Fandom Is Ugly: Networked Harassment in Participatory Culture*. New York University Press.

Sun, Meicheng. 2020. "K-Pop Fan Labor and an Alternative Creative Industry: A Case Study of GOT7 Chinese Fans." *Global Media and China* 5 (4): 389–406. https://doi.org/10.1177/2059436420954588.

Sun, Taiyi, and Quansheng Zhao. 2022. "Delegated Censorship: The Dynamic, Layered, and Multistage Information Control Regime in China." *Politics & Society* 50 (2): 191–221. https://doi.org/10.1177/00323292211013181.

Tencent. 2021. *There Are So Many Subcultures, Why Are Fan Circles So Crazy?* Assessed August 20, 2024. https://news.qq.com/rain/a/20210926A08R7P00.

Thimsen, A. Freya. 2022. "What Is Performative Activism?" *Philosophy & Rhetoric* 55 (1): 83–9. https://muse.jhu.edu/pub/2/article/855141.

Trottier, Daniel, Qian Huang, and Rashid Gabdulhakov. 2024. *Digital Media, Denunciation and Shaming: The Court of Public Opinion*. Routledge.

van Dijck, José, and Thomas Poell. 2013. "Understanding Social Media Logic." *Media and Communication* 1 (1): 2–14. https://doi.org/10.17645/mac.v1i1.70.

Wang, Di, and Sida Liu. 2021. "Doing Ethnography on Social Media: A Methodological Reflection on the Study of Online

Groups in China." *Qualitative Inquiry* 27 (8–9): 977–87. https:// doi.org/10.1177/10778004211014610.

Wang, Erika N. 2022. "Squid Game outside the Wall: Fandom Nationalism in China and Negotiation with State Power." *Communication, Culture & Critique* 15 (4): 549–51. https:// doi.org/10.1093/ccc/tcac038.

Wang, Erika N. 2024. "Participatory Censorship with Illusory Empowerment: Algorithmic Folklore and Interpretive Labor beyond Fandom." *Social Media + Society* 10 (4): 1–16. https:// doi.org/10.1177/20563051241295800.

Wang, Erika Ningxin, and Liang Ge. 2023. "Fan Conflicts and State Power in China: Internalised Heteronormativity, Censorship Sensibilities, and Fandom Police." *Asian Studies Review* 47 (2): 355–73. https://doi.org/10.1080/10357823.20 22.2112655.

Wang, Eureka Shiqi. 2022. "Contested Fandom and Nationalism: How K-Pop Fans Perform Political Consumerism in China." *Global Media and China* 7 (2): 202–18. https://doi. org/10.1177/20594364221093768.

Wang, Yan, and Ting Luo. 2022. "Politicizing for the Idol: China's Idol Fandom Nationalism in Pandemic." *Information, Communication & Society* 26 (2): 304–20. https://doi.org/10.108 0/1369118X.2022.2161827.

Wang, Yiming, and Jia Tan. 2023. "Participatory Censorship and Digital Queer Fandom: The Commercialization of Boys' Love Culture in China." *International Journal of Communication* 17 (March): 2554–72. https://ijoc.org/index.php/ijoc/article/ view/19802.

Wang, Zhe. 2018. "'We Are All Diba Members Tonight': Cyber-Nationalism as Emotional and Playful Actions Online." In *From Cyber-Nationalism to Fandom Nationalism*, edited by Hailong Liu, 53–71. Routledge.

Warner, Michael. 2021. *Publics and Counterpublics*. Princeton University Press.

Wellman, Mariah L. 2022. "Black Squares for Black Lives? Performative Allyship as Credibility Maintenance for Social Media Influencers on Instagram." *Social Media + Society* 8 (1): 1–10. https://doi.org/10.1177/20563051221080473.

Wu, Geer, Jinzhang Jiang, and Xueying Wang. 2025. "Dual Exploitation and the Long Tail Effect: The Affective Labor of Chinese Real

Person Slash Fan Production." *Television & New Media* 26 (6): 719–35. https://doi.org/10.1177/15274764251324474.

Wu, Xiaoping, and Richard Fitzgerald. 2024. "Internet Memes and the Mobilization of a 'One-China' Cyber Nationalist Campaign: The Case of the 2016 Diba Expedition to Taiwan." *Social Semiotics* 34 (4): 697–719. https://doi.org/10.1080/10350330.2023.2183113.

Wu, Xu. 2007. *Chinese Cyber Nationalism: Evolution, Characteristics, and Implications.* Lexington.

Xu, Jian, and Ling Yang. 2021. "Governing Entertainment Celebrities in China: Practices, Policies and Politics (2005–2020)." *Celebrity Studies* 12 (2): 202–18. https://doi.org/10.1080/19392397.2021.1912109.

Yang, Guobin. 2019. "Performing Cyber-Nationalism in Twenty-First-Century China: The Case of Diba Expedition." In *From Cyber-Nationalism to Fandom Nationalism: The Case of Diba Expedition in China*, edited by Hailong Liu, 1–12. Routledge.

Yang, Ling, and Yanrui Xu. 2016. "The Love That Dare Not Speak Its Name: The Fate of Chinese Danmei Communities in the 2014 Anti-porn Campaign." In *The End of Cool Japan: Ethical, Legal, and Cultural Challenges to Japanese Popular Culture*, edited by Mark McLelland, 163–83. Routledge.

Ye, Weiming, and Luming Zhao. 2023. "'I Know It's Sensitive': Internet Censorship, Recoding, and the Sensitive Word Culture in China." *Discourse, Context & Media* 51: 100666. https://doi.org/10.1016/j.dcm.2022.100666.

Ye, Zhen, Qian Huang, and Tonny Krijnen. 2024. "Douyin's Playful Platform Governance: Platform's Self-Regulation and Content Creators' Participatory Surveillance." *International Journal of Cultural Studies* 28 (1): 80–98. https://doi.org/10.1177/13678779241247065.

Yin, Yiyi. 2020. "An Emergent Algorithmic Culture: The Data-Ization of Online Fandom in China." *International Journal of Cultural Studies* 23 (4): 475–92. https://doi.org/10.1177/1367877920908269.

Yin, Yiyi, and Zhuoxiao Xie. 2024. "Playing Platformized Language Games: Social Media Logic and the Mutation of Participatory Cultures in Chinese Online Fandom." *New Media & Society* 26 (2): 619–41. https://doi.org/10.1177/14614448211059489.

Yoon, Kyong. 2023. "K-Pop Trans/Nationalism." In *Routledge Handbook of Asian Transnationalism*, edited by Ajaya Kumar Sahoo, 394–405. Routledge. https://doi.org/10.4324/9781003152149-36.

Zhang, Chi, and Yiben Ma. 2023. "Invented Borders: The Tension between Grassroots Patriotism and State-Led Patriotic Campaigns in China." *Journal of Contemporary China* 32 (144): 897–913. https://doi.org/10.1080/10670564.2023.2167054.

Zhang, Qian, and Keith Negus. 2020. "East Asian Pop Music Idol Production and the Emergence of Data Fandom in China." *International Journal of Cultural Studies* 23 (4): 493–511. https://doi.org/10.1177/1367877920904064.

Zhang, Weiyu. 2016. *The Internet and New Social Formation in China: Fandom Publics in the Making*. Routledge. https://doi.org/10.4324/9781315756141.

Zhang, Weiyu. 2024. "The 30 Years of China's Online Fandom." *Communication and the Public* 9 (4): 421–5. https://doi.org/10.1177/20570473241270576.

Zhang, Xiaoyu, Delia Dumitrica, and Jeroen Jansz. 2024. "Mapping Chinese Digital Nationalism: A Literature Review." *International Journal of Communication* 18: 1891–912. https://ijoc.org/index.php/ijoc/article/view/20767.

Zhang, Yuan, and Ralph Schroeder. 2024. "'It's All about US vs THEM!': Comparing Chinese Populist Discourses on Weibo and Twitter." *Social Media + Society* 10 (1): 1–18. https://doi.org/10.1177/20563051241229659.

Zhao, Andy, and Zhaodi Chen. 2023. "Let's Report Our Rivals: How Chinese Fandoms Game Content Moderation to Restrain Opposing Voices." *Journal of Quantitative Description: Digital Media* 3: 1–35. https://doi.org/10.51685/jqd.2023.006.

Zheng, Xiqing. 2024. "Chinese Media Production and Fandom between Queerbaiting and 'Survival Instincts'." *Media, Culture & Society* 46 (7): 1437–53. https://doi.org/10.1177/01634437241241964.

Zhou, Kui, and Weishan Miao. 2019. "Contested Visual Activism: Cyber-Nationalism in China from a Visual Communication Perspective." In *From Cyber-Nationalism to Fandom Nationalism*, edited by Hailong Liu, 109–24. Routledge.

Zhuang, Yuyi, Songge Huang, and Chao Chen. 2023. "Idolizing the Nation: Chinese Fandom Nationalism through the Fangirl Expedition." *Chinese Journal of Communication* 16 (1): 53–72. https://doi.org/10.1080/17544750.2022.2108861.

INDEX